Communication Skills Training

How to Talk to Anyone, Connect Effortlessly, Develop Charisma, and Become a People Person

PUBLISHED BY: James W. Williams

Table of Contents

Your Free Gift

As a way of saying thanks for your purchase, I wanted to offer you a free bonus E-book called ***Bulletproof Confidence,*** exclusive to the readers of this book.

To get instant access, just go to:

https://theartofmastery.com/confidence/

Inside the book, you will discover:

- What are shyness & social anxiety, and the psychology behind them

- Simple yet powerful strategies for overcoming social anxiety
- Breakdown of the traits of what makes a confident person
- Traits you must DESTROY if you want to become confident
- Easy techniques you can implement TODAY to keep the conversation flowing
- Confidence checklist to ensure you're on the right path of self-development

Introduction

Thank you for purchasing this book, *Communication Skills Training: How to Talk to Anyone, Connect Effortlessly, Develop Charisma, and Become a People Person.*

By purchasing this book, you understand how much of an impact communication has on your daily life. From the transactions you complete to the more intimate moments, the way you convey your thoughts and feelings will determine how much people will interpret it.

Having been working in various industries for years and meeting people from all walks of life, I have found out that communicating your thoughts, feelings, and ideas is highly important for a lot of reasons. Whether you only want to close important deals or build long-lasting relationships, the ability to communicate is something that must be developed.

For some people, good communication skills are seemingly second nature. They have no problems telling people what is on their mind and have the same generally be positively accepted by anyone listening to it.

As a result, you could see notable examples of people easily building connections and generally succeeding in their endeavors. One simply needs to speak their thoughts, and others seemingly listen. You might have even heard of people so charismatic that they can even make huge social movements or be generally well-liked by everyone in a building.

For most people, the skill has to be learned and honed. And most likely than not, you belong in the latter group. If you are the type of person who has always been misinterpreted or have difficulties even expressing themselves, then this book is the cure to your predicament.

Everything you will learn here is based on a combination of years of research and personal experiences and is supported by factual and empirical data. You might encounter an abstract concept or two, but rest assured that all of the information you will get here can be applied in actual day-to-day scenarios.

What you have to understand is that communication skills, like any other ability in the world, has to be honed. Nobody becomes a charismatic person who can speak to a lot of people in a matter of hours.

More often than not, they started where you are right now: not quite sure how to do things, but having a clear goal of what needs to be done in order to improve.

And since it needs training, you need to take a look at different aspects that revolve around it. You see, communication is not just about talking. It involves picking the right words to say, combined with the right temper to convey the right message.

Communication is also not just about the things that come out of your mouth. The way you carry yourself in public and give off non-verbal cues can also lend a hand in making people understand what you are trying (or not trying) to say better.

Part of the process would also include identifying the basics of communication. With this, you will also identify the mistakes commonly made by people in communicating thoughts and ideas. You might even have committed these yourself, which negatively affected several interactions.

And, of course, communication is not a one-way thing. In as much as you are trying to convey a message, you must also learn how to interpret the verbal and non-verbal messages given to you by the people that you encounter daily.

Listening is also one skill that you must learn. You might be surprised to find out that the ability to process information being directed at you is just as important as clearly conveying your thoughts and ideas. But listening is not enough. You also have to do it in an empathetic and attentive manner to carry a conversation.

And speaking of conversations, it is also important for you to understand that you must adapt your communication style to different people. Remember that everybody has their way of perceiving things and their own set of priorities in communicating. As such, you have to find out how you can make yourself be heard to different personality types in a way that is conducive to effective communication.

One other thing you will also learn is how you can effectively communicate your thoughts and ideas in different formats and scenarios. There are challenges presented in each, and it is necessary for you to overcome these challenges and effectively convey what you are thinking and feeling with the tools at your disposal.

However, you will also realize that not every conversation is going to go as smoothly as possible. There is always that chance that you will fail in conveying your thoughts and ideas effectively, or even process information the way that a speaker wants you to do so.

You will learn how to deal with a breakdown in communication and try your best to veer back on course. Aside from this, you will also learn why communication can fail, which may be due to the inherent barriers set up by people or other external factors.

One other aspect you will also learn is how to deal with your emotions, anger especially, and still be an effective communicator. More often than not, we let our emotions run over us, which can be potentially damaging to our relationships. However, there is a way to manage such passionate feelings and still be as polite and diplomatic as ever.

In conjunction with that, you will also learn how to deal with different “difficult” conversations and people as well as build rapport with total strangers. After all, one of the goals of communication is to establish a connection with those around you.

So, is there a point in improving the way you communicate? The answer is yes. You will also learn throughout the book of some great examples of communication and form your own actionable strategies to improve the way you speak.

These are just some of the things that you will learn about communicating in this book. If you have no further questions or hesitation, now is the time to jump into the world of communication.

Let’s get started!

Chapter 1: Some Basic Considerations

"Half the world is composed of people who have something to say and can't, and the other half who have nothing to say and keep on saying it."

-Robert Frost-

Before we go into the more exciting stuff, we should cover the basics first. Considered as one of the most valuable interpersonal skills right now, communication helps you share information from one person to another and multiple people at once.

There are many ways and styles to communicate, and what you may be using right now is perfectly valid (albeit with some necessary tweaks here and there). But it would be best that you try to discover how crucial it is to properly communicate your thoughts and feelings to others as well as interpret those being directed at you.

The Importance of Communication

So what is the point of trying to improve the way you communicate and interpret things? What you may not have realized is that communication is involved in almost every aspect of your life.

Have you ever had those moments when people were able to get what you were saying without technically saying anything at all? A mere nod of your head or how you grip another hand in a handshake can give lots of messages, depending on the context of the situation.

Or how about when you talk to three different people at the same time, and they end up reacting differently to what you just said? You told them the same thing, and yet one was happy, another became confused, and another was potentially offended. Why is this so? It goes back to the receiving part of communications, and people often react differently to the same stimulus.

The point is that communication helps you share ideas, build relationships, close potentially rewarding transactions, manage a group, and delegate tasks. If anything has to do with interacting with another living, breathing being, you can be certain that such a situation will rely heavily on your existing communication skills.

The Types of Communication

Regardless of your approach to speaking your mind, all forms of communication will fall under four distinct categories:

1. Verbal

This is perhaps the one that is easiest to understand as it is the one that you are going to use a lot regularly. Verbal communication involves your mouth and your brain. Nothing else.

However, its sheer simplicity is also what makes verbal communication one of the trickier aspects of communicating your thoughts and feelings. Without the proper tone, body language, and mood, you could easily end up being misunderstood by what you just said a few seconds ago.

This aspect of communication also has the widest range of styles. Some people are so verbose that you'd think you are talking next to a humanoid thesaurus. Others are curt and blunt, getting straight to the point, damn all the consequences. And then some can take too long to get to their main message because they digress.

Learning how to make your style compatible with others will help you a lot in becoming an expert in verbal communication.

2. Non-Verbal

This is where all physical gestures and cues will fall under. Also, the facial expressions that you use to convey what you are verbally communicating will be included here as well. For example, smiling while telling a story gives the impression that the information you are about to offer is good to listen to.

What makes non-verbal communication so crucial is that your ability to pick them up and understand them will help you adjust your behavior in any situation. For instance, a potential client of yours is crossing his arms, and this could tell you that they are not sold on what you are saying and need further convincing.

Alternatively, the tapping of feet is a telltale sign that the person is in a hurry to cut the conversation and go somewhere else. A relaxed position, on the other hand, could tell you that the person might be agreeable to anything that you might propose. For now, at least.

3. Written

Technically speaking, written communication is also non-verbal, but it has some qualities that warrant it being its own class. Written communication involves every act to include writing, typing, or printing text and symbols onto something physical and digital.

Out of all the forms of communication, this is the one that is most tangible as it is seen through books, pamphlets, blogs, emails, memos, letters, and other printed mediums. Consequently, this is the type of communication that has a sense of permanency as the things that you wrote can be, figuratively speaking, set in stone.

For instance, Sun Tzu has been dead for over a millennium now, and yet, *The Art of War* is still being printed and read in different languages. The same goes for Shakespeare, Plato, Newton, King David, and even the Founding Fathers of America.

Because written words tend to last longer than you and might even represent your legacy to younger generations, you must be as accurate with it as possible.

4. Visual

Out of all the forms of communication, this is perhaps the most artistic. The phrase "a picture paints a thousand words" is highly applicable here as one image can tell very different messages for every person looking at it, depending on their mood in that instance.

The visual medium is often used to support your words by providing context. Let us say that you are telling your superiors that sales figures for the past few months have been subpar. Wouldn't it help your case if you had something like a pie chart that would give your listeners a visual anchor point to better understand your words?

But, even on its own, visuals can convey messages that could help someone make a connection with what they have seen and what they are feeling. As such, careful use of images is key to a lot of fields, especially advertising.

What Good Communication Skills Can Bring to You

If communication is a major part of your day-to-day living, then improving your skills will yield you several benefits, which will accompany you through all the different facets of your life.

1. Trust Building

Learning how to properly convey your thoughts and feelings can be a good foundation where you can build trust with others. An ability to listen intently to whatever one person is telling you and seeing things from their perspective gives the impression that you are making decisions not only for yourself but for everyone else.

By being an active listener, you also make the people around you comfortable enough to be open with their thoughts and feelings. This fosters an atmosphere of trust, especially in relationships that require the performance of obligations and duties or collaborative effort.

Here is a classic scenario: If you are the team leader and your team is about to make a decision, the most sensible thing that you can do is to let others air out their concerns and provide alternatives. Then, once all concerns, issues, and alternative routes are presented, the team votes on which decision the entire group is going to take.

Sure, the final decision will not satisfy everyone, but, at the very least, you provide people on your team with a forum where they are free to speak their minds and be listened to. This is a far better option than a "It's my way or the highway!" approach to decision making where nobody else can dictate the actions of the team but you.

2. Solving Problems (and Preventing Them)

It is often said that problems exist because of pure miscommunication. There is no shortage of examples out there of a falling-out between groups or destruction of public images just because one person conveyed their thoughts and feelings poorly.

Here is a scenario: Let us say that one of your friends just got a makeover for a special event. When you see her, what would be the most sensible thing to say? Would it be "Why, you look lovelier today!" or "Hey, I never knew you could be this pretty!"? If your answer would sound something like the latter, then you tend to inadvertently generate conflict where you go.

Meaning well, yet being misunderstood, is a problem that most face. But learning how to be tactful with your words does help iron out issues that you have with others and prevent them from occurring again in the future.

3. Clarity and Direction

A good communicator knows how to provide clearly-defined expectations, objectives, and ideas to the people they are talking to. This is quite helpful in group efforts, where a clear line of communication between members is necessary.

Suppose that a member is not performing up to standard. A good communicator will know how to tell them that they need to get back on track without offending them. It is all too easy for a person to get angry and bite at the people they think are lagging. With good communication skills, on the other hand, you can help people understand what they need to do in the most diplomatic way possible.

Of course, fostering an open line of communication between group members helps in eliminating conflicts and misunderstanding. Perhaps one team member is about to get into a fight with another member. With good communication skills, you can intervene and give them a place where they can talk things out (with you as the mediator). This way, you can address issues that your team faces and get back on track to finish the task as quickly as possible.

And clarity does not only work with group efforts. Being clear requires you to be at your simplest and most direct when it comes to talking. This means you can tell people what you are trying to say in a few words or less with no digressions at all.

Doing so helps people get the message behind what you are trying to say without wasting time deciphering your monologue. After all, nobody likes to start a conversation with someone who takes five sentences to answer a simple categorical question.

4. Better Relationships

Perhaps the most direct benefit of improving your communication skills is that you can easily build or maintain interpersonal relationships. After all, you can now speak effectively, tactfully, and openly, which gives the impression to people that you are a person that has nothing to hide. Transparency, after all, is a quality that is hard to manifest unless you know how to say the right thing at the right time and using the right words.

Not only can you speak well, but you also learn how to listen to others. This gives the impression that you are also considerate with how other people think and feel and, in turn, respect differences in opinions. This would foster a relationship built on mutual trust and respect.

5. Reading and Responding to "Cues"

You might be surprised by this, but not everything that is ever conveyed to you will be 100%. This is quite true in tense and stressful situations where the things not said can dictate how things would happen as much as the things that were said in public.

And it also does not help that some personality types are difficult to handle by default. A pushy salesman, an angry boss, a detail-heavy mechanic, a mother who is stuck in traffic and is driving her kids to soccer practice. All of these require you to pick up on non-verbal cues in order to respond with the right words.

A bit of awareness of the body language of others can give you a great advantage when closing deals and finding solutions for problems. Also, it helps you adjust the tone of your verbal message so that it fits the overall mood of the place and the mentality of the people listening to you.

Here is a good example. Suppose you are delivering a lecture and notice that most of the class is tuning you out because your class is boring. You can inject humor or draw from your life experiences to get the attention of everybody as jokes and personal stories can make people connect to what you are saying. With good communication skills, you can pay attention to how people are reacting to your message and adjust your delivery accordingly.

6. Improving Productivity

Once the hindrances towards proper communication are done with (more of them on a later chapter), everybody around you knows what you can do and will find you a more reliable person. This is effective in group efforts as, now, members can get the idea that they don't have to do everything just to complete a task.

With good communication, workloads can be distributed quickly, conflicts settled before they get out of hand, and you can deal with your stress in the most direct yet diplomatic manner possible. In essence, by communicating better, you get things done as soon as possible, which makes you a more productive person overall.

7. Making a Good Impression

Presenting yourself can be a rather nerve-wracking experience. Even if you have well-prepared material for your presentation, the execution of your plan can be derailed if your nerves get the better of you.

One good skill you will learn in improving your communication is how to deal with what is effectively called "stage fright." Learning how to manage your nervousness before going in front of people and conveying your thoughts assertively and authoritatively can make you a far more convincing speaker.

Presentation also involves how you can recover from any mistake without losing stride in front of everyone. This will include learning how to turn your mistakes into something humorous to endear yourself to the public and also cut off dead air in your presentation.

All in all, good communication skills can allow you to present your message in a way that is attractive and yet easy to understand.

The Qualities of Good Communicators

As was stated, communication is a skill that must be developed over time. Practice is what eventually elevates you from a less than efficient communicator to a good one.

The end goal of becoming a good communicator is to make everyone who is involved in a conversation feel like their contribution to it will matter. And in order for that to happen, a communicator must possess a certain set of skills.

1. Active Listening

Knowing how to form your message is one good skill, but a more important one is to receive those messages being directed to you. Instead of interrupting other people or taking away the focus from that person to them, a good communicator focuses on what is being told to them.

Listening intently and letting the other person finish is also not enough. A good communicator also understands the value of letting the person talking confirm that their message is being received and processed. Through nods and other short non-verbal messages, a communicator tells the speaker that they are tuned in to the conversation.

This would help in preventing conversations from becoming monologues while also helping a person with a problem find the most effective solution for it.

2. Empathy

There is this misconception that communication needs to be mired with protocol and politically-correct term usage in order to be effective. This only makes conversations stiffer for the participants and, in some cases, artificial.

Instead, a good communicator will seek opportunities wherein meaningful dialogue can take place, and collaboration is assured. These can only be made possible if they truly understand where the other person is coming from and how they view certain issues.

Rather than force their own opinions into a certain matter, a good communicator will understand how people feel in a certain situation and adjust their approach accordingly. This is quite essential in negotiations or even in building cordial relationships with others. If you are not the person that can see things from perspectives other than your own, or learn how to adjust in situations, then you need to acquire these skills to be an effective communicator.

3. An Open Mind

To assume is a human tendency, but this can often lead to conflicts. For instance, you might think that a person is dominating the conversation when it is just his natural way of speaking. Or what if you assume a person to be shy or timid just because he does not talk a lot?

Either way, assuming too quickly can be detrimental in conversations as it leaves space open for future conflict. A good communicator will clarify things first and seek to get the most basic information right. This way, the message that they are about to deliver gets perceived in a manner that they intended for it to be perceived as.

4. A Positive Mindset

Enthusiasm can be a rather hard emotion to maintain, especially if one is already used to being cynical. However, it can also be an effective tool in engaging with people as it naturally makes them excited for what is to transpire in the conversation.

Offsetting negativity is a key quality good communicators have since a few negative comments are all it takes to derail an entire conversation. By rallying people to their cause and making them excited for what is about to happen next, a good communicator can teach people to be motivated and even resilient when the tougher times come.

To Summarize

The truth is that communication is a rather simple concept to follow. You do not need to even have a higher level of learning to be a good communicator. All it takes is for you to have the right mindset and approach to get the best benefits of being a good communicator.

Now, in a perfect world, the conveying of thoughts and ideas follows a rather simple path and would lead to a beneficial conclusion. But we aren't living in a perfect world, are we?

So why do our day-to-day communications seem, for lack of a better word, flawed?

Chapter 2: Why We Don't Communicate Right

"The single biggest problem in communication is the illusion that it has taken place."

-George Bernard Shaw

In as much as it can be easy to get communication right, it is also equally easy to get things wrong with it. Sadly, the latter is more likely to happen in one's day-to-day.

There are quite a lot of reasons why a lot of our conversations can get derailed in a matter of a few seconds and several poorly-worded statements. And surprisingly, there are quite a lot of them that you have encountered for yourself on a regular basis.

The Barriers towards Effective Communication

Man, whether he is conscious of it or not, has several barriers erected around him that would prevent messages from being interpreted the way they should be.

By identifying what these barriers are, you are one step closer to improving your communication skills. After all, what is there left to do with a barrier that you identified than to, well, smash it?

1. Physical Barriers

This is the one easiest to spot because it depends on actual physical conditions in the environment. For instance, you are trying to talk to a person, but they are several meters away from you. Or what if you are trying to talk to somebody in a crowded, noisy room?

Even the layout of an office can serve as a barrier to effective communication. Cubicle walls, for example, can absorb a lot of noise, which prevents workers from talking to each other unless they stand up and talk with each other over the wall.

And, of course, faulty equipment is a physical barrier, especially in remote communication. A broken microphone or a sudden weakening of the Internet connection can cause messages to be distorted, preventing listeners from interpreting a message properly.

Fortunately, being easy to spot means that physical communication barriers are the easiest to solve. If one can't hear you because you're too far away, you get closer to the listener. If the walls in your office are preventing communications, you talk over them. And if your communication equipment is faulty, then you invest in newer and more reliable ones. And so on and so forth.

2. Language Barriers

A barrier of the linguistic one is something that you will also encounter often but is a bit trickier to deal with. The fact that each region of the world has their own preferred set of languages can be a barrier to effective communication because two people may not know how to talk to each other in one language that both know.

"But isn't English the universal language now?" you might ask. That is true. Ever since the world has become globalized, many countries have adopted English as the standard for international communications.

But here is the thing: English is not the same in one country over another. For instance, the kind of English used in America is completely different from the one used in Britain or Canada. The same goes for other continents that have their own colloquial terms used in conjunction with English words.

On a more local scale, there are the dialects that change from one region to another or, more accurately, once every few thousand kilometers. Of course, some nationalities speak English with a rather thick accent.

Included here are the different linguistic styles. Some people speak in a simple and yet direct manner while others are very verbose and use highfalutin words. And then there are those professions who encourage people to talk at an advanced level of English like law, academics, and science.

As a result, in one modern neighborhood, you can find more than three dialects, accents, and linguistic levels being used in daily communication.

3. Psychological Barriers

This is one of the more insidious barriers as you will not know that they exist until they manifest themselves. The most common psychological barrier is stage fright, where you experience massive nervousness before speaking in front of several people. If overwhelmed by their nerves, the person may even experience difficulty delivering a single sentence clearly.

But there are far more potent psychological barriers being erected around people out there. These include depression, speech disorders, phobias, and other deep psychological problems that limit one's ability to speak clearly.

In most cases, some psychological issues collaterally affect your speech only. This means that fixing them must be done not only to improve your communication skills but to improve your mental health as well.

4. Emotional Barriers

Although closely related to psychological barriers, emotional barriers have a shorter lifespan. In other words, they are barriers only because your emotional state at that moment made them so.

A strong emotional quotient allows a person to communicate effectively and perceive messages the way their speaker intends for them to be received. However, high emotional states can affect your way of receiving messages.

For example, anger and sadness can make a person interpret a message negatively. On the opposite side of the spectrum are happiness and contentment, which makes a person even more receptive to messages.

5. Cultural Barriers

A more recent barrier faced by people is the exposure to different cultures coming from different nations. It cannot be helped that one culture is different from yours, and such differences can be manifested by the way you communicate with them.

People coming from reserved, isolationist cultures tend to speak only when spoken to while those coming from more open and highly social cultures tend to be easy conversationalists.

There are also other cultural factors to consider like a religious practice or lack of one, sexual identity, diet, preferred pets, and overall general behavior. And this might even surprise you, but cultural factors will also dictate the type of topics you can expect to talk about when it comes to certain cultures.

As such, it is a must to take into consideration the differences in cultures when communicating with other people. You cannot assume that they will perceive things the same way as you do due to these differences. This is the very essence of being culturally appropriate.

6. Attitude Barriers

The way that a person is predisposed towards interpersonal interactions will also determine how well they communicate with others. Introverts like to be left alone and thus shy away from most verbal communications and physical contact. However, they might excel in remote communications like online chatting.

And then there are those personality types that are social or clingy. Of course, there are personality types that could be perceived as blunt and inconsiderate or egotistical and domineering. All of these could play into how you can communicate with people. Under the right conditions, they could even serve as an impediment to you getting your message across properly.

7. Organizational Barriers

This barrier is commonly seen in places where there is an organizational structure. Here is a scenario: have you ever wanted to talk to a person but feel hesitant because they are one rank or several ranks higher than you in the company's organizational chart? That's an organizational barrier.

Or what if you wanted to tell a person something but can't because company protocol demands that you do not disclose sensitive information to people that are lower in the chart? That is an organizational barrier right there.

Admittedly, a lot of companies are doing away with the rigidity of the organizational charts and employ a more transparent line of communication between people regardless of their position. This means that how much the organization's structure can impede communications depends greatly on the culture of that group.

One Important Reminder: Although these barriers are prevalent, it does not mean that you will have to face all seven of them even in your lifetime. If you are the person who has never traveled to another country, you may have never had a linguistic barrier problem. And if you do know how to circumvent them, physical barriers might not even be a problem for you.

Also, the magnitude of the problems that one faces is different from another person. Your psychological barriers might be minor compared to another person, but you might have more problems dealing with organizational barriers than those around you.

The point is that knowing what barriers you have to face in your communication skills is the key to finding a way to discover a creative workaround for problems they might pose.

Busting Some Misconceptions

As with any other skill out there, it is easy to build your communication skills on the wrong foundations. Such foundations are based on some misconceptions regarding the art of conveying your thoughts and feelings to others or perceiving the same. As such, we must correct such wrong information in order to proceed properly.

Myth 1: Listening Skills are not Needed

This myth is based on the notion that communication is simply the relaying of your thoughts and ideas to another person and nothing else. As such, you only need to learn how to craft your message to be a good communicator.

But the truth is that it only makes you a good talker, not a communicator. Listening is an essential skill to learn, as it helps you form your words in response to how people are feeling or most likely will receive your message. In essence, good listening skills help you refine your message and make it resonate with whoever you are conversing with.

Myth 2: Sharing of Information is the Same as Communicating

The truth is that communication is always a dialogue, not a monologue. This means that more than one person is involved, and a back and forth of responses are to be expected if an interaction is to be labeled as a conversation.

As such, communication focuses on the two sides between participants, which means that a considerable focus is put on how you can maintain a healthy conversation with people. In other words, your ability to read non-verbal cues, process responses, and adjust your way of talking accordingly are crucial skills in become a better communicator.

Myth 3: You Must Only Share the Message in One Way for Optimum Effect

Here is the thing about humans: they won't get what you are trying to say at once. This is dependent on whatever barriers they have inadvertently erected for themselves that prevent such a message from being processed properly.

As such, you need to find ways to make your message reach out to a lot of people. This can be done by finding the right platforms where you should air out your message as well as the type of form it will take. For instance, if you have a good speech, you can convert into text form for easy reading or make it a supplement to a lecture.

It's up to you to find out how you can keep your message "evergreen" for as long as possible. And, fortunately for you, there are ways to convert your message from one format to another (which will be discussed later on).

Myth 4: Constant Communication is Always Good

Sure, talking regularly is one way to improve your skills. After all, practice makes perfect.

However, as with all things, the best signifier that you have improved as a communicator is not quantity, but quality. There are a lot of people out there that talk a lot without saying anything meaningful. And then there are those who say important things but keep repeating them.

Frequency is also a matter that you need to figure out in delivering your message. Say it too many times and it might become annoying; say it sparingly and it won't have an impact. The right amount of repetition for your message, while also keeping its form diverse enough, should help in making whatever you are trying to say last in the minds of listeners for as long as possible.

Communication Mistakes (and How to Avoid Committing Them)

Communication is labeled as a competency. This only means that the skill is best gauged not through conceptual, abstract means, but through actual application.

And there lies the problem. With application comes the tendency to make mistakes, and humans are particularly known for their tendency to commit mistakes. For communication, these mistakes can either be substantial or formal, but they will most likely affect your interactions negatively. As such, identifying them is crucial if you want to improve your skills.

1. Not Exactly Listening

The most common mistake people make in communicating is giving it the bare minimum of effort while giving the appearance of paying attention. When somebody is talking, you might be busy going through your phone or writing something or watching the television. Worse, your mind is wandering off to somewhere else, so everything being relayed to you does not even register in your brain.

This is problematic on two fronts. First, it makes the person talking feel invalidated as you are unintentionally shutting off whatever they are trying to convey to you. Second, it makes you miss out on important non-verbal cues being displayed, which makes you run the risk of misreading the entire situation and giving an improper reply.

The only remedy here is to give your full attention to the speaker, which is one of the crucial skills you will learn later on.

2. Interrupting the Speaker

We have all done this. How often have you cut off a person mid-sentence since you think you know what they are going to say next? For instance, a person might be telling you what just happened to them, but you just butt in and say, "get to the point already!" That's a rather rude thing to do, and it stops any momentum that the speaker is building on.

An even worse thing that you could do is interrupt the speaker and then interject your own story. Not only did you cut the momentum of the story off, you just took the attention away from the speaker to you.

Interrupting a person mid-sentence is often seen as a power move, but it's a rather discourteous one at that. The end result is that you are invalidating the person as if telling them subtly that whatever they are trying to say does not matter.

This can be remedied with a bit of courtesy. You have to learn when a person has stopped talking, which tells you that it is now time to respond.

3. Assuming the Message

This often happens between friends since this mistake is dependent on how well you know that other person to act and think. When a person is trying to speak, our minds are already formulating assumptions as to what they are trying to convey to you or, at the very least, their intentions behind such.

More often than not, the assumption is wrong. This only becomes a problem, however, if you make the assumption manifest by performing mistake number two or giving the wrong response.

When one assumes what a person is trying to say, they miss out on the person's true message. Maintaining an open and curious mindset in regards to the speaker and his message should solve this problem.

4. Emphasizing the "Incorrect" Nouns

You might be surprised by this, but the nouns that you use in your message can be determined by the tone of that message. Let us say that you are trying to address a problem in front of your team.

So, more often than not, you would use the nouns "you" so everything you are going to say next falls along the lines of "You didn't do this," "You should have done that," or "You did this."

The "you" statements are often uncomfortable to listen to as they feel like personal attacks. This makes the listeners form negative connotations about what you are trying to say to them, resulting in miscommunication.

A more cautious usage of your words is necessary here. Instead of using "you" statements, you should use "I" and "we." The latter two are more inclusive and lean towards personal accountability. With these, you can soften the blow for any message that you would try to convey, especially serious ones.

5. Being an Emotional Responder

Emotions are good for making sure that you adjust your responses in accordance with the situation. But what happens if you let your emotions run over you? More often than not, you are going to say things that you don't mean and would regret later on.

There have been far too many instances of people saying stuff that bring with them serious interpersonal consequences just because they were sad, angry, or emotionally distraught. One crucial skill you will have to develop, then, is to let your emotions run through you while still picking the right words to say in response to any person talking to you.

The key here is to not say anything when your emotions are at a high. For instance, if you are extremely angry, it is best to let the anger burn through you before you do anything. You may even vocalize your frustrations, but just make sure that you don't vent it out on somebody you'd rather not want to hear you rant and rave.

And, of course, a little bit of restraint can go a long way here. Even if you have a social media account, do not use it as a diary where you channel your anger. Things often said online have a tendency of coming back and doing some serious damage to your credibility.

6. Plain Misinterpretation

More often than not, human beings fail to properly interpret messages. Perhaps it is because of the barriers listed above, perhaps it is because of our emotional state upon receiving the message, perhaps it is because of our lack of skill in perceiving the different nuances of a message.

Whatever the case, we perceive the message in a manner that is not intended by the speaker. This is even more prevalent with modern-day technology when other elements like voice, tone, and non-verbal cues are done away with. Even the ability to detect sarcasm and condescension is harder with the Internet nowadays.

This problem is often avoided if you pay full attention to what is being directed at you. This involves more than mere listening as you have to analyze what is being said, how it is said, and what other non-verbal messages were accompanying it.

There is no assurance that you will perceive the message 100% correctly, depending on the situation. However, you can be certain that your response will be a better-informed one if you take the time to listen and analyze.

7. Being Vague

This might be in response to the need to not accidentally offend other people nowadays, but becoming too vague or subtle in your communication is a rather ineffective style. The reason for this is that vagueness always leaves wide room for interpretation.

An all-too-common example of this is when we feel upset and post something rather vague on Facebook. When pressed for more details, we talk in the vaguest of terms possible. In some cases, we use a passive-aggressive tone just to mask the fact that whatever happened has gotten to us on an emotional level.

If you are not careful, you may end up having wildly different interpretations of something that could have been otherwise simply understood. Worse, you may be perceived to be talking without actually saying anything.

The only remedy here is to not beat around the bush. Be as direct as possible while maintaining a level of courtesy with the way you convey your thoughts and feelings. You cannot expect people to read your mind, so do not make that a requirement in conversing with you.

8. Not Accounting for Cultural Differences

Even if both parties speak at the same level of English, there are minute differences in the way that they convey thoughts and feelings. Cross-cultural conversations are often hard because not everyone gives the same verbal cues. They don't even mean the same thing for one word, depending on the region.

One great example of this is between American and British English. For starters, both have different sets of idioms and colloquial terms. Next, they have different tones and approaches, with the British being perceived as more formal and verbose while Americans are seen as curt and simple.

Either way, failing to account for key differences in term usage, sentence structure, and non-verbal cues can lead to miscommunication between parties.

Again, the solution here is to make things as plain as possible. Use a level of language used by all and try not to impress others with advanced words or idioms that are not used by the general public. The point with communication, after all, is to express and not to impress.

9. The Ad Hominem

When you do not like what a person is saying, the most common thing that humans do is to attack the messenger. This often happens in informal debates when the person starts looking for defects that are observable in the person instead of any logical flaw in their argument.

The reason for this is rather simple: character flaws are easy to spot and can derail an otherwise well-structured conversation with minimal effort. On the other hand, it is a telltale sign that you no longer have anything valuable to offer to the dialogue.

As such, we often hear things like "You're just an (insert politician's name here) supporter!" or "Why should I listen to a (insert political party/race/social status here)?" easily thrown by people nowadays. It's a way of ending a difficult conversation, but it is one that does nothing in improving your credibility as a conversationalist.

The only way to prevent yourself from committing a mistake of this kind is to stick to the facts contained within the message. Make sure that your arguments are responsive to what was being directed at you and not merely hostile by default. You have to realize that you may not agree with the person on principle but, at the very least, you can respect their views while also presenting your own in a manner that is not offensive to all.

And speaking of difficult conversations....

10. Deflecting or Delaying

When faced with the prospect of conveying difficult subject matters, we often make the mistake of prolonging the conversation for as long as possible. Perhaps you'd rather not be scrutinized over something you have done or know of. Or perhaps you can't find the words to tell everybody else of something they would not like to hear.

As such, you resort to veering off the issue so that you won't be placed in a position where you will become the bearer of bad news. The problem with this, however, is that it only makes matters worse in the long run.

Careful management of tension is key to telling people what they must hear without creating conflicts or damaging relationships. A bit of tact and proper selection of words would also help you in this matter.

Timing is also necessary for delivering your message. You must not wait too long when delivering the news, but you must not rush things through until you have all the information confirmed. This way, you can craft a message that is going to be received by all in the best manner possible.

Either way, you must not withhold information to protect the feelings of others at the expense of telling the truth. In the most mindful and diplomatic manner, of course.

In a Nutshell

There is no denying that the path of the message from its source to its listener is fraught with many obstacles. These obstacles might not exactly impede the message from being received, but it does affect how the person receiving it responds.

Fortunately, most of these obstacles, mistakes, and other barriers towards effective communication can be addressed and corrected. This means that, with training, you can slowly correct the flaws in the way you communicate and prevent yourself from committing the mistakes listed above. That is, of course, if you commit to constantly improving your communication skills.

Chapter 3: The Art of Active Listening

"I remind myself every morning: Nothing I say this day will teach me anything. So if I'm going to learn, I must do it by listening."

-Larry King

Surprisingly, one of the most important tools that you need to develop in your communication skills is not your mouth. It is those two things that lie on either side of your head.

The concept of listening sounds rather simple and straightforward. All you have to do is receive the sound waves coming from a person's mouth and have your brain interpret what those waves are carrying. And so as long as you have a perfectly healthy (and clean) set of ears, you are bound to be a rather decent listener.

But to truly be listening in the sense that you get the essence of what the other person is saying to you is often hard to pull off. Conversations are tricky, after all, as they fraught with nuances, innuendos, non-verbal cues, and other hidden messages. And there are topics out there that are hard to interpret if you do not give it your undivided attention.

It is at these moments that you have to learn how to understand a person, even if they are not sure of what they are trying to say to you. This is where you will apply what is called active listening.

What Exactly is Active Listening?

The most basic explanation of active listening is that it is the kind of listening that involves the use of one's full concentration. The goal of this type of listening is to understand the person delivering the message.

By understanding, it means to delve deeper into their message and find out what exactly they are trying to say. This does not only include the words that they use but the emotions and the body language that accompanies such.

Using this type of listening, you are expected to form the most appropriate response to what had just been said to you. At the same time, you have a better chance of recalling fully what you just listened to.

The premise of active listening is that it paves the way for a clear exchange of thoughts and feelings. This, in turn, would increase the chances of you coming to an understanding of every person involved in a single conversation.

One key element necessary to make active listening possible is empathy. This is the ability to see things from the perspective of other people, even if you do not agree with them in principle.

With this quality, active listening is made possible, especially in three critical areas.

1. Empathetic Understanding

The most basic aspect of active understanding, this simply involves listening while also trying to perceive things similarly to how the other person perceives them. In essence, you are subtly telling the person that you understand what they are saying and also understand what they mean and are feeling right now.

2. Listening Without Agreeing

If you understand where that person comes from, does it mean that you have to agree with them? No. It simply means that you now understand their perspective and can formulate a response that counters that without disrespecting the person on a personal level.

In essence, you can now tactfully share your viewpoints while respecting the differences that other viewpoints have with it.

3. Willingness to Listen

This aspect covers your readiness to listen to what a person is saying with ***no distractions at all***. This is the more challenging part as there are quite a lot of distractions that could prevent you from listening to that person fully. This includes your busy schedule and the devices that you surround yourself with.

This also includes fighting all urges to pretend to listen. This is not only rude but runs contrary to the basic concept of actively listening to another person. If done all too frequently, you run the risk of damaging relationships, personal or otherwise.

The Steps towards Active Listening

Active listening is a skill which means that you have to develop it over time. To do this, here are some steps to help you make yourself an active and effective listener.

1. Eye Contact

When you talk to a person and you try your best to avoid meeting their eyes, this is a telltale sign that you are not giving the conversation your full attention. This includes constantly checking your watch or phone, scanning the room, or looking out the window.

Most Western countries value eye contact as a basic foundation for active communication. This is quite important as certain conversations can take a while to get finished. If you are not comfortable locking eyes with the other person, you invite all urges to get up and move.

As such, when a person is speaking to you, put everything unnecessary down. If you are typing something at your computer, stop it. If you are writing something down, stop it. If you are eating, for the sake of the conversation and to prevent yourself from choking on your food, stop it.

"But what if the person does not want to make eye contact?" There are some cultures out there where eye contact is either discouraged or subtly not recommended. This includes some parts in Asia and the Middle East.

If the other person finds it hard to make eye contact, let them be. Stay focused on your gaze to lock in your attention to the conversation at hand.

2. Relax

There is a difference between making eye contact and staring fixedly at the person. You can always look away and maintain a mindful awareness of your surroundings since this is a basic human instinct.

Being "attentive" can mean a lot of things. This includes being present at the moment and giving most, if not all, of your attention to the object in front of you.

The goal here is to actively maintain focus while tuning out all distractions, like noise and activity, in the background. Lastly, do not let yourself be distracted by your feelings, biases, and other inner trains of thought. Your mind must be open enough to let information come through from the conversation so that you can respond appropriately.

And speaking of your mental state...

3. An Open Mind

It is often part of human nature to make a mental note of the person's distinct features and mannerisms when they are talking to you. For instance, if they say something incredulous, your mind immediately makes a mental note along the lines of *well, that was a stupid thing to say,* followed by an instinctive raising of the eyebrows.

Or what if the person has a visible distraction on their face like a mole on their cheek or a piece of lettuce in their teeth? Your eyes would immediately travel there, and your focus is now on the "fault" and not on the messenger.

Either way, indulging in mental criticisms in the middle of a conversation will impede your ability to effectively listen to the other person. As such, you must listen without making any hasty conclusions.

Always remember that the person, despite their mistakes, is doing their best to relay what they are thinking and feeling. If you don't listen, you will never get to what they truly want to say to you.

Also, it is at this point that you must correct your tendency to hasten the person in finishing their narration. You may be the type of person who wants to speed conversations up or are just bothered with people beating around the bush. Whatever the case, do not cut a person off so they can get to the point at their own pace.

4. Visualize

The best way to retain and process information in your brain is to convert that information into a "mental image" of sorts. This could be a sequence of abstract things forming a narrative or even an actual mental picture, but the image helps you keep focus on what the person is saying.

This is rather important, especially if the person is relaying to you a narrative of events leading to an incident. That narration could go on for several sentences and paragraphs, which takes a while to get condensed in your brain without some mental aid.

Your mental picture can be a sequence of mental images, or abstract things, or even keywords. The point is that it will help you formulate what to say next.

But here is the kicker: while you are listening, you must not spend even a fraction of your time planning what to say next. The mind is not designed to listen while also rehearsing your response internally at the same time. While listening, your one and only focus should be the things the other person is saying even if they happen to be rather boring.

5. Avoid Interjections

When we were young, we were most likely taught that it's a rather rude thing to interrupt people who are talking. Despite what modern media is telling you (i.e., that in-your-face, confrontational behavior is good), being rude and obnoxious during conversations will always lead to an aggressive put-down, verbal or otherwise.

When you interrupt a person, you can convey a lot of messages, which include "My story is more important than yours" or "I do not have time for you." What you have to understand is that people think and feel at very different paces.

This means that the burden of adjusting to the speaker's pace is, well, on you.

And even if you do not wish ill, you can be an interrupter if you tend to provide a solution when it is not solicited. Think of it this way: if that person is seeking your advice, they would gladly ask for it once their narration is over.

If not, then refrain from giving unsolicited advice. More often than not, people just want a person to listen, and not a solution. But if you do have a brilliant idea, always ask the speaker if they want to hear it. But only do this once that person has said their piece.

6. Wait for the Stop

How would you know that a person has stopped their narration? It is easy to say that this is the moment when their jaws stopped flapping, but there is an actual "pause" that you have to look for, the intangible "stop" that signifies you that a sentence or paragraph has ended.

The stop happens when a person does not add anything else after a second or so of not talking. You could even tell in certain people that they are not about to add anything else because they do not visibly catch their breath as if winding up for another paragraph of narration.

Once the stop has occurred, you can then present your response. Or, better yet, you can ask the person to go back on some details, especially the ones that you were the most confused with.

This makes for a perfect segue with the next step, which is...

7. Maintain Course

Picture this scenario: Your friend has just been talking to you in the last few minutes about a wonderful experience he had at the last Superbowl season. You, in all of your meticulousness, zeroed in on the part of the story where he was sitting next to an acquaintance of yours that you hadn't heard from since 2010.

Then you asked, "Oh, you were sitting next to Bobby from way back in high school? How is he? I heard he's going through a rough divorce. It must suck for the kids."

Question: Was what you just said relevant to his Superbowl experience, or did you just unconsciously veer the conversation into somebody else's personal life?

If you answered the latter, then you at least know that you unconsciously committed one of the biggest mistakes in communication: changing the topic. The things that we say right after a person is done talking have, more often than not, nothing to do with what they just said. It takes a while to get back on topic, but it is easy to derail an entire conversation this way.

If you know that you have an annoying tendency to do this, you have to learn how to veer back to the primary topic. After the person is done answering what you just asked, say something like, "Oh, that's hard to hear coming from Bobby. But tell me more about your Superbowl experience. It was great, right?"

In just a few sentences, you just shifted the focus back to the speaker's topic with them none the wiser for it.

8. Step in their Shoes

As the person speaks, you might notice that their emotions would start to surface. This is good as emotions are rarely hidden, especially if the person is talking about something personal.

What you have to do here is synchronize your emotions with that of the speaker's. If they are joyful, show joy. If they are fearful as they describe what is troubling them, show concern.

A key element here is to make your reactions visible through the words you say and the expressions you show. And this is where empathy can help you as it allows you to see things from that person's point of view. It takes concentration and time to master, but it will eventually help you become an effective listener and communicator.

9. Give Feedback

It is not enough that you see things from that person's perspective or understand what they are feeling. You also have to visibly confirm to the speaker that you are listening.

There are multiple ways to do this. The easiest one is to vocalize your reactions with phrases like "Wow, that's wonderful!" or "I'm sad to hear about that," or "That sucks. I can see why you're frustrated!"

But what if the person's message or feelings are unclear or you don't know how to react out of fear of being misunderstood as indifferent? You can easily confirm that you are paying attention by nodding or using filler words like "mm-hmm" or "uh-huh."

The goal here is to assure the speaker that they have your undivided attention and that you are following their narrative. This is important in situations where the person is not only telling a story but giving you instructions for performing certain things.

10. Pay Attention to What *Isn't Said*

Email notwithstanding, most of the direct forms of communication you will regularly encounter is non-verbal. There are a lot of things that a person can tell you without opening their mouth. It is up to you, then, to know how to pick up on these non-verbal cues.

Here's a good example: When somebody talks to you over the phone, you might wonder how to tell if they are happy or not. Listen for the tone they use whenever they start the conversation.

If it is a happy one, you can be 75% sure that the rest of the conversation will be a lighthearted one. If you detect a sense of seriousness in their tone, you could be certain that what they are about to tell you is urgent. And so on.

These non-verbal cues are even more pronounced in face-to-face conversations. If you are that astute, you can even detect things like boredom, irritation, and even sarcasm coming from the other person as well as obvious facial expressions. These are things that any person could not ignore, which is why you should consider them when responding to what the person has just said.

Some Exercises to Improve on Your Listening Skills

Active listening is something that you would not develop overnight. It takes time and practice to master in order to be an effective listener. To do that, here are some exercises that you could implement in your daily interactions.

1. Paraphrasing

Most of the time, it is hard to process a lot of information in one passing. Chances are that you won't get everything that the person has said, which means that your response is going to be far from good.

So, how could you make them repeat what you just said without giving the impression that you were not paying attention? You paraphrase.

How this is done is easy: you only have to repeat what they just said or what you understood about the situation and ask for a clarification at the end.

A paraphrase should sound like this: "So, you (the speaker) just had (insert situation here), and you would like to (insert their question or proposition here). Is that right?"

More often than not, the speaker would indulge you by clarifying certain details of their story without going through everything again.

Paraphrasing is also good for summarizing all their key points, which keeps the conversation going. If a person is angry at something you did, you can zero in on that point of their narrative and say something like, "Would you like to hear the reasons why I did that?"

Or what if a person made an observation? You could follow it with a question like, "Are you referring to (information A) or is it (information B)?"

Paraphrasing works not only to clarify any detail in the speaker's story, it also helps the person collect themselves and reorganize their thoughts. In either case, you and the other person have a better chance of reaching an understanding.

2. Words to Avoid

Reacting to what has just been said is important. However, we often make mistakes when responding to the message. All of this can be traced back to our instinct to have the problem solved instead of actually listening to the person.

Here are some of the responses that you should try your best to avoid saying when a person is speaking:

- Telling a story: "That happened to you, too? That reminds of that time when..."
- Pitying the person: "You poor thing..."
- Correcting them: "Uh, I don't think that's how it went..."
- Comforting them: "I know it's hard, and none of this is your fault...."
- One-upping the person: "You think that's bad? What happened to me was worse!"
- Cutting them short: "Uh, I'd love to listen more. Can we do it later?"

What you normally say when in a conversation might be different from the ones above. Either way, you should identify your response gaffes so you would know which ones to avoid when talking with other people.

3. Your Own Non-Verbal Cues

Listening to what isn't said works just as much on yourself as it does on the speaker. What are your usual ticks when listening to a person while he's talking? List them down and find out whether or not they help the conversation or harm it.

For instance, crossing your arms while a person is talking can be perceived as you being uncomfortable with either the message or the speaker. The same is true when you constantly tap or shuffle your feet or make a loud clicking noise when a person is talking. It signifies that you would rather be somewhere else.

As such, you have to identify which of your non-verbal messages are hostile, or could be potentially perceived as hostile, and find ways to minimize doing them when in front of people. Doing so could make the conversation that follows easier for you and the other person.

What Makes Active Listening Hard?

The truth is that active listening is not the easiest thing to perform at all times. If it were, then a lot of miscommunication would be avoided, which, as far as your personal experiences can be gleaned upon, is far from the truth.

As such, you have to identify where you could also make a mistake in trying to be an active listener. Here are three areas to consider:

1. The "No Solution" Stance

The biggest issue with active listening is that people, by default, are problem solvers. Some fields and disciplines have this mentality so hardwired that it becomes hard for people in those areas to become effective listeners.

How hard is it, you ask? Here's a classic example: Let us say that a friend of yours is telling you that one of their family is sick with something serious like cancer. As they are narrating their story, you are already coming up with suggestions like where to get treatment, dealing with the complications, and managing the stress.

What you are not doing, on the other hand, is listening to the narrative. You fail to get the context of the story or even understand the intention of the person relaying this information to you. In your haste to provide them with solutions, you fail to reach an understanding with the person.

Arguably, it is your eagerness to solve problems that should be dealt with the most in learning how to actively listen. That is not to say that providing advice is not good (it is), but you should get the context of the story first before you start doling out advice.

2. Dealing with Tough Emotions

If the subject is rather personal, emotions are expected to run high. Like the example above, you can expect the person telling you their story to start tearing or choking up. This is a sign that their emotion for the story is still raw, and they are visibly hurting from even relaying it to you.

The first impulse with people, however, is to find a way to make the person stop crying. Perhaps you might say something like, “It’s okay. Don’t cry!” or try to change the topic. The reason for this is rather simple: it is rather uncomfortable to see a person display strong emotions. In some cultures, being emotionally expressive is even seen as a sign of weakness.

Either way, a lot of people are not designed to cope with the emotions of others, let alone their own.

The biggest challenge that you would face here is to embrace the emotions being directed at you, no matter how hard it is. It is essential to let those feelings be seen and heard for you to respond appropriately.

3. Dealing with the Silence

Being silent is often uncomfortable in a conversation. While you are refining your skills, you might even allow entire seconds of silence to go by before the conversation resumes. In most cases, those periods of silence can be awkward for you.

However, dealing with those periods of silence is but part of the process of becoming an active listener. What matters more is that you visually confirm what has been relayed to you by your own emotions and the expressions you make.

You can cut through the silence with the clarification or paraphrase to help the other person relax. This could also give the impression that you are trying to understand them and were paying attention to their story, thus validating themselves before your eyes.

The key here is timing. You have to hone the ability to detect pauses and stops in the person's narration of events. Once you identify when these occur, you can then add to the conversation without coming off as rude or impatient.

To Conclude

If we were to summarize the active listening process, it would look something like this:

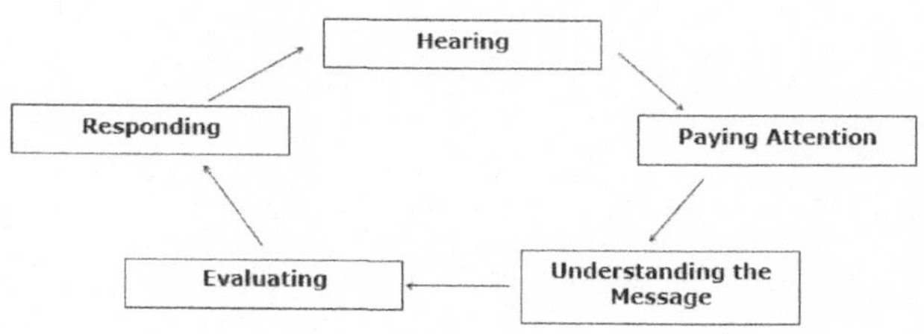

Sounds simple and straightforward, right? That's because it is.

The only thing that you have to remember in order to be an active listener is to fully invest yourself in the conversation. Allow nothing else to distract you from receiving the message and its context so that you can mold the best possible response.

Of course, it takes time to develop this skill, which means you must constantly engage in conversation to improve as an active listener. Sure, you will make mistakes down the road, but you will eventually learn how to listen first before acting or responding.

Chapter 4: The Basics of Interpersonal Communication

"Communicating to a relationship is like oxygen to life. Without it....it dies."

-Tony Gaskins-

Connecting with others is a valuable skill. If you look at the history of humankind, you will find little examples of people who managed to live on their own. Sure, you might know of a few examples, but they are mostly under dire circumstances.

And unless you're stuck in a rock or lost in a miles-long tundra, you are bound to meet other humans in your day-to-day living. And with this high probability of near-constant human encounters comes the need for constant interaction.

Mingling with other people should not be a difficult concept. But you might be surprised at how a lot of people screw up on the basics of interpersonal communications. As such, here is a refresher of sorts to help you enhance the way you can communicate with other people. And this is regardless of how they think and feel from you.

The Different Personality Types

The biggest hurdle that you will face with communicating your thoughts and ideas are the very walls that people have set up themselves from all outside elements. The biggest of these so-called "walls" is their own personality.

To keep things simple, how a person communicates and processes information is different depending on their personality type. Your ability to find a creative workaround through each personality type can help you effectively communicate with that person without necessarily changing how they think, feel, and perceive things.

To do this, you must first get acquainted with the DiSC system for personalities. Just keep in mind that understanding the DiSC personality profiles is not a surefire success in improving your interpersonal relationships and communication. It is just there to give you a baseline understanding of how one person could be different from another.

1. D for Dominant

Personality styles under this profile are hardwired for one thing only: results. They are fast-paced individuals who aim to achieve at all costs.

As a consequence, they tend to be strong-willed and forceful. On more negative terms, they could be pushy and domineering. A D-type personality tends to act fast and is eager to see changes resulting from their actions.

Due to this, D-types are also highly opinionated and expect everybody else to follow along with their pace. At worst, they could come off as blunt and uncaring and can border on recklessness.

However, their results-driven personality means that they don't waste too much time feeling sorry for themselves, especially if they make a mistake (which is highly likely given their "act first, think later" style). They can also be visionaries, focusing on the bigger picture while also motivating others to do their best.

2. I for Interactive

These set of personality types are perhaps the most outgoing and interactive among the four personality profiles. They are primarily designed to be as social as possible.

Because of this, I-types are not as detail-oriented as other profiles, nor are they too keen about working on their own. However, like the D-type, I-types are as fast-paced and oriented towards getting things done. They only want to make sure that everybody is in the same car before starting their trip.

I-types thrive on being liked and, as such, don't take too nicely towards being rejected. As such, they would rather not deal with people who tend to be as abrasive or confrontational when it comes to dealing with others. And this fear of being the pariah tends to make I-types make sure that everybody has had their say before making any decision.

When under stress, the I-type becomes too talkative or emotionally disorganized. They also have a tendency to promise something but fail to follow through it.

However, their greatest strength is maintaining high spirits, which can be motivational for others. They also are rather great in starting discussions with people, which easily makes them catalysts for great ideas. And, more often than not, I-types are considered as the proverbial "glue" that keeps everyone within a group connected.

3. S for Stable

This is perhaps the most laid back of all the personality types. They are mostly described as even-tempered and supportive as they also value collaborative effort, equality, and a bit of justice.

Stability is the main goal of S-types, which makes them the least accepting of personality types towards changes in the status quo. S-types are also constantly needing reassurances from their peers, especially when approaching new challenges and situations.

This overly-cautious approach towards change makes S-types one of the “slower-paced” personality profiles out there. They are the ones that take the longest to decide on something and might take a while in elaborating any information to listeners. However, this has an upside: if an S-type decides to do something, nothing save for divine intervention will stop them from completing their task.

Under pressure, an S-type becomes supportive, but that can easily become too enabling or, worse, smothering. As a matter of fact, S-types tend to sacrifice personal creature comforts just to diffuse conflicts and help everybody settle.

4. C for Cautious

The most detail-oriented personality profile out there, C-types are known for their intense passion for getting things right on the first attempt. C-types are the ones that tend to have the highest possible personal standards and work ethic in any group, although it is not uncommon for them to lower their expectations and deal with how things are right now, not how they are supposed to be.

C-types are meticulous to a fault. When relaying their ideas, they would rather make sure that whatever they are saying leaves no room for interpretation. Every possible argument has to be preeminently shot down, and any contradiction corrected or, at least, explained.

As such, it is common for C-types to go into these long, complex, and tangent-heavy explanations, which will require a lot of time to process and respond accordingly. They are not the ones that do well with being criticized or even corrected, which they often see as a personal attack.

Outwardly, C-types can be too critical and can offer unsolicited advice. As such, people tend to only talk to a C-type or involve them in discussions only when it is truly necessary.

However, you must understand that C-types are aiming not to improve a person but, rather, a system. Their attention to detail and commitment to excellent performance would make any C-type the designated expert of a group.

Talking with the Personality Types

Right at the get-go, you would already have an idea as to how you would approach the different DiSC profiles just by looking at their general description. Either way, your goal should be about synchronizing with how they think and perceive in order to have your message be received by them the way you want it to be received.

D-types want things fast and with little to no fluff. As such, you are better off being direct when talking with them. Get to the point within the first few sentences and minimize filler words like "um," "like," and "sort of." And if you do want to correct them, be as direct as possible as these profiles can take that feedback. The less you waste their time, the more you get in their good graces.

For I-types, you would want to come off not as intense but still high-spirited. The trick here is to let them make a move first. If they are happy, you must respond in kind with a happy remark. If they propose something, do not hesitate to affirm or build on it by contributing your own ideas.

For S-types, you should take your time to communicate with them. If you are proposing something new and radical, your best approach to these people is helping them see things from a logical standpoint. Explain to them all possible consequences coming from such a decision to make them see things from your perspective. You have to assure them that whatever new challenge they are about to take is within their ability to complete.

As for the C-type, it is best that you be as careful with them as possible. You must develop an ability to diplomatically relay information that prevents the C-type from seeing it as a personal attack. You also need to be as detail-oriented as them, dealing with facts and figures over abstract concepts.

In all four personality profiles, your strategy is the same: empathize with how they think and feel, and see things from their point of view. You cannot browbeat them or force them to adopt new ways of thinking. What you can do, instead, is mold your message to fit their personal biases.

If done right, you should be able to build a strong—or at least functional—relationship with different personalities.

Establishing Rapport

Maintaining good relationships is a worthy goal. But what about building them in the first place? You might find that it is easier to maintain a connection with the people that you already know as opposed to welcoming new people to your personal or professional life.

However, that can be hard as changes in your life will force you to meet new people and establish contacts. As such, you have to know how to build rapport with the people around you. And here's how:

1. Managing Self-Worth

The first hurdle you have to clear here is how you view yourself. And the problem can go in two ways. It is either you think too highly of yourself or too lowly.

If your problem is the former, you have to always consider the fact that you are not infallible. Any idea you can contribute or opinion you air out can be corrected or enhanced further by the people around you. In essence, you must not put yourself at a level above others to shield yourself from criticism.

If your problem is the latter, then you must train to believe that you are worthy of being communicated with. You should remember that you are worthy enough to share your ideas and even challenge ideas that run against what you believe in.

Why is managing your self-worth crucial in building rapport? The answer is that how people treat you will be directly or inversely proportional to the way you view yourself. If you think too highly of yourself, people will automatically try to put you in your place. If you think too lowly of yourself, well, you are just giving people the consent to run you over in every interaction.

But viewing yourself as an equal to everybody around you allows for a clean slate of sorts where you can start building on relationships. An even-keeled view of yourself tends to make the act of building rapport easier.

2. Be Genuine

The best first thing that you can do in building rapport is to present yourself as you are. You don't have to adopt a new persona or even sound like a salesman when presenting yourself.

So what does it mean to be genuine, then? It only means that you present yourself the way you are. Of course, you'd have to be presentable and behave yourself in public, but you have to make sure that all your interactions are founded on the most genuine version of yourself.

If you are the one to burst out laughing at jokes, do so. If you are the one that loves to be loud and jovial, do so. Just relax, smile, and go with the flow in any social gathering. Just make sure that you address the more abrasive aspects of your personality before you meet other people, however.

3. "Tell Me About Yourself"

It cannot be avoided that people can get defensive when being asked something personal. This is a common thing to happen when you are talking with a stranger.

However, you can diffuse tension right from the start if you ask a person to tell you more about themselves. This technique has a twofold effect. First, it helps ease the person by signifying that you are there to make a connection with them. The more at ease they are, the less defensive they will get when you prod more.

Second, it helps you learn what is important to them by their own words. The request is a rather broad one, after all. When a person talks more about themselves, they subconsciously reveal tidbits of information that can help you smooth out the conversation as it progresses. This also goes well with the next tip, which is...

4. Finding Shared Humanity

As you learn more about that person, you will find out that you and they might share the same interest in certain things. Perhaps they like golf and reading like you do. Perhaps they are into deep-dish pizzas like you. Or perhaps they think that the Golden State Warriors are the best NBA team now like you do. And so on.

The point is that there are some commonalities you share with that other person, which allows you to connect with them. This is rather important as you would have to remember that everyone within one room is totally different from one another. Perhaps others have bigger savings on the bank, others have multiple degrees, and others have an intimate knowledge of car engines, and so on.

But, at the very least, everyone can relate to each other by what they like or don't like. Use these shared interests and viewpoints as a foundation of sorts for any potential relationship you will build.

5. Mind Your Body Language

Your non-verbal messages also play a role in you establishing rapport. For starters, your hand gestures—from the firmness of your handshake to the things that you do with your hands while a person is talking—can tell them whether or not you genuinely want to be left alone in their presence.

The way people react with hand gestures is hardwired to our evolution as our caveman ancestors often gauge how threatening another human is by what is in their hands.

To be seen as non-threatening, keep your hands at a comfortable distance from your body but make them as relaxed as possible. This means that you should not conceal your hands inside your pockets or fold your arms.

One foolproof way to make yourself less intimidating is to simply mirror what the other person is doing. If they are relaxed in their chair, be relaxed in yours. If they are eating while conversing, do so as well.

This is a rather helpful trick for you as your focus shifts from trying to make an impression to blending in with the general mood of the room. You will be surprised to see how many non-verbal cues you can pick up if you are not too overly cautious with your body language.

6. Tone Matters

The way you say things can also lend a hand to your impression of other people. A loud and booming tone is often seen as either boisterous or confident, while a quiet and softer tone is seen as shy and reserved.

This is also important, especially when you are responding to other people. If you tend to shout out your words, you are perceived as a person who lacks control. But if you are too soft-spoken, then you are perceived as someone who generally lacks confidence.

As such, your only solution here is to be aware of your tone and voice. If you are not sure what tone to use in a situation, use something calm and collected. This is vital in business meetings and important deals.

The FBI has been using the calm and collected voice to diffuse high-tension situations like a hostage-taking. By lowering their voice to something calm and non-threatening, they tend to help in calming the hostage-taker, so they don't do something drastic. Use this voice when approaching potential contacts to give the impression that you are in control without being domineering about it.

7. Always Project Confidence

It is human nature to gravitate towards people who are passionate, positive, and confident. It is the first thing that people often look for when searching for friends or, better yet, suitable life partners.

In the first few seconds of meeting, you will be judged as either an equal, an inferior, or a superior depending on your confidence. So, how do you project confidence? It is all in how you carry yourself. A confident person has an upright statute with shoulders down, chest forward, and chin up. The hands are also visible as if welcoming a person.

As for eye contact, it should be straight and can lock gazes with another person within two to three seconds after meeting them. And then there is the assertiveness of how you say things. In essence, you must speak your mind in a manner that is clear and forceful without being too intimidating.

One good example here is when then-presidential candidate John F. Kennedy appeared in a series of live debates again then-incumbent President Richard Nixon. JFK exuded confidence and was rather smart and articulate in all of his responses. His charisma was to the point that he was the more presidential-looking candidate out of the two. Nixon, for some reason, looked pallid and fumbled through his lines. Eventually, JFK's impressive performance in his public appearance won him the Presidency.

Something to Remember: Like everything else in this book, building rapport takes practice. For your projection, you can practice in front of your mirror. Rehearse some lines and responses in advance and address any flaws you might spot as you speak. If done right, you should easily endear yourself with people in a room minutes after meeting them.

Humor and Why it Works

You have seen countless examples of people gravitating towards an individual who can tell jokes. All they need is one punchline and boom, they have endeared themselves to ten or twenty people.

So why is humor a rather effective tool in any human social interaction? Surprisingly, the answer lies in biology.

When the brain detects something stimulating like humor, it sends signals to the body to release endorphins all throughout the body. Endorphins are pheromones that do a lot of things, but the one that is most relevant to conversations is that it helps the body relax and feel good. And when the person feels good and is relaxed, they are more open to any suggestion or proposition.

In practice, here's how it works: imagine that the person you are talking to just had one of the worst days of their life. Their car got towed, the neighbor's dachshund just dug another hole in the backyard, and to top it all, they overcooked their sausages, so now they have to settle for stale cereal for breakfast.

And here comes you, with another thing that might add to their burden. Perhaps it's just you telling them that their mail was sent to your address or that you want to borrow some money. Chances are that you will be rejected way before you can even say something.

However, if you come to them in a manner that makes them lighten up for just a bit, then your overall presence around them would be more welcomed. The same goes for interpersonal relations. With humor, you can diffuse tense situations while also making your presence a valuable one within any group.

And this does beg the question: How do you become a natural jokester? Here are a few tips to help you with that.

1. Know When and What to Joke About

When it comes to jokes, there is acceptable humor, and then there is offensive humor. When diffusing situations, you might opt for the kind of humor that offends the very least.

Take the time to analyze what kind of humor works in that situation. You need to determine whether or not you should be cracking jokes in that situation.

Of course, this does not mean that vulgar jokes do not have their place in any group interaction. Doctors and lawyers, for example, are down with some nasty jokes given the nature of their work, but the same could not be said for younger folk.

You only have to make sure that whatever you are going to say next is going to be received positively in any situation that you are in, especially statements that were supposed to lighten up the mood.

2. Be Subtle About it

You will have to understand that there is intelligent humor, and then there is low-brow humor. In any given situation, you'd rather stick with the one that is impactful and relevant, which is why you'd pick the former over the latter.

Intelligent humor does not mean that you must start quoting smart shows like *Rick and Morty* or *Monty Python* to be funny. It is all about finding a way to inject your jokes into conversations as if they were a natural part of it. It also helps if you could come up with an observational, on-the-spot quip there to help the other person feel at ease (if they need to, of course).

3. Curb that Inhibition

Surprisingly enough, one key trick that helps you become an effective communicator will also help you in becoming a bit more humorous: get rid of that shyness. This is where your confidence as a person will come into play as you have to deliver the punchline in one single stroke.

The best kind of jokesters out there are those that can deliver one good line and can recover from a bad one without fumbling over their lines or stammering.

Of course, you have to practice on your line delivery in order to get good at it. But just remember that funny people are rarely shy, and those that are often use their shyness as a punchline. Whatever your style, you should have enough confidence to say what you want to say and maintain a straight face while doing it.

4. Get Some Inspiration

Here's a secret comedians wouldn't want you to know: Most of them were inspired by previous generations of comedians. The *Monty Python* crew inspired the writers of *South Park* and Eric Andre while Red Foxx and George Carlin can be considered as the predecessors of the likes of Dave Chappelle and Bill Burr.

The point is that humor does not have to be original to be funny. Chances are that your audience has yet to hear about that joke, so it's okay to use some lines. After all, people will remember you more for the connections you made and less from the jokes you cracked. Just make some changes here and there to be relevant to the topic at hand.

Networking Tips

The natural consequence of learning how to interact with people is that you end up making important connections in every aspect of your life. A network, if you will, that will help you get the resources and information you need to achieve more out of a single day.

Maintaining one is rather easy as long as you are agreeable and know how to convey your thoughts and feelings politely. It's in building one where the challenges are usually located. To build your network, there are a few tips that you have to keep in mind.

1. Make a Good First Impression

The impression that you leave on introducing yourself to people can determine how successful you can be in starting a relationship with them.

For starters, you have to look the part. Look like someone that people would love to communicate with at first glance. Second, you have to freshen up on your social skills. Just don't do anything that will give people the idea that you are sloppy and messy by default.

2. Practice Your "Elevator Pitch"

The elevator pitch is a technique that salespeople use to promote themselves and their products within seconds after meeting a person. It doesn't have to be something elaborate, but what is necessary is for you to lay out the essential information about yourself within a minute or so.

It could look something like this:

"Hi, I'm (state your name). I'm a (state your credentials). I've noticed that you are (state something that you noticed about the person). I have been (state your experience). Maybe we could talk about this matter more. Here's my number (give your business card if you have one). I look forward to hearing from you."

Within a minute or so, you would have told that person who you are why they should start a relationship with you. This one takes practice, but you are bound to engage in conversations without leaving your would-be contacts confused or annoyed.

3. Avoid Small Talk

Small talk is something that should be reserved only among friends and colleagues. It is something that should not be the core topic of your conversation with a would-be contact.

More often than not, you will encounter networking opportunities in meetings, conferences, and other events. As such, you should be doing plenty of research before heading to these events. And if you do meet that contact on a chance encounter, just pay attention to what they are saying. Your conversation with them is bound to yield a lot of information that could be helpful to you.

4. Pull Out

You just had a rather productive conversation with a potential new friend. Now what? Your ability to excuse yourself out of any conversation would matter here because nobody is ever going to tell you that this conversation is over at all times.

You can make up any excuse like you having to go to the bathroom or moving to another group to see another friend. All of these are valid, so long as they give the people you meet the subtle hint that your dialogue with them is over.

And avoid "dead air" where you and that person you were talking to stare at each other, saying nothing for entire seconds. Once you excuse yourself, go in the general direction of where you said you were going.

The Bottom Line

Creating those bonds is easy if you break everything down to their most basic components. Different people have different ways to perceive things and relay such information to you. This means that any conversation could go anywhere, depending on what you are and the kind of people that you are talking to.

Conversations involving the same topic can go differently, and that depends on the overall mood of the room. You can use this to your advantage by learning how to defuse tensions or just give off a confident and welcoming vibe.

Remember that just because you have an inkling of how people think and feel, it does not mean that your conversations with them would go 100% smoothly. There is always that chance of failure and misunderstanding, depending on how you carry yourself and come into the conversation.

Either way, your primary strategy towards interpersonal communications is always the same: Adjust to the things around you and not the other way around. You must be flexible enough to change some elements in your approach while still being confident enough to carry yourself out of any situation in the most direct manner possible.

If done right, you should come out of any conversation successfully. And by successfully, that means getting what you want out of the conversation while also building relationships that could last for as long as humanly possible.

Chapter 5: Dealing with "Noise" Part I: Communicating When Angry

"Between what is said and not meant, and what is meant and not said, most of love is lost."

-Khalil Gibran-

In a perfect world, we only have to say what we are thinking, and everybody understands us. Better yet, everybody is in the right mood to receive messages and respond in a way that is healthy and conducive to a healthy conversation.

But we don't live in a perfect world now, do we?

More often than not, you will encounter situations where the chance of miscommunication is quite high. All it takes is one poorly-worded response or a blazing temper to derail a conversation, preventing you and the other person from reaching an understanding.

Why is this so? To answer that question, let us break down the concept of communication into its basic elements.

Let us say that communication is a network of nodes comprised of several connections, namely:

- Source
- Sender
- Medium
- Receiver
- Outcome

In practice, the source gives a message to the sender who then relays it to the receiver via their chosen medium, like verbal, written, or electronic. The receiver then interprets the message, which results in the conversation generating an outcome.

However, here is the problem: In the nodes of the sender, medium, and receiver lies a certain element called "noise." How great this noise's influence is in each node will determine the outcome. If the noise is too great, then the outcome is miscommunication or misunderstanding. If not, then it results in an understanding.

The process can be further simplified in the following table.

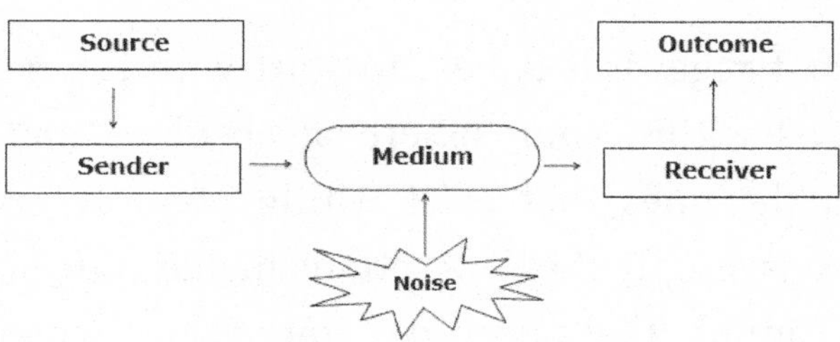

So what's the noise in the medium that ruins your chances of a successful communication opportunity with people? It can take on many forms, and this chapter will be dedicated to identifying the most egregious ones you will regularly encounter.

Dealing with Stress and Anger

First things first—when we talk about noise, we are not talking about that physical auditory barrage of sounds that hinders your ears from hearing anything important. At least, not technically.

Noise is something that can effectively disrupt the transmission of information between the sender, the medium, and the receiver.

In that regard, it is best to start with the noise that is within your sphere of absolute control (i.e., the ones that exist within you.) Internal noise is simply the distractions inside your body and mind that prevent you from properly processing external information.

Internal noise can include something as simple as being tired or having an upset stomach or becoming drunk. Any change in your body is undoubtedly going to impede the way you communicate, think, and feel.

But, in this regard, it is best to deal with the most common and intense internal noises: stress and anger.

Being under pressure is a universal feeling among humans. However, it does change the way we communicate and, for most of the time, it is for the worst.

On the flip side, no good has ever come out of suppressing your anger and frustrations. Instead, you should learn how to act on feelings of anger and stress in more positive ways. Here are a few tips to remember.

1. Change Your Perceptions

The thing with anger and stress is that everything is so raw that it only takes one small push for you to blow up. Under stress and intense anger, people tend to become overreactive.

Here's an example: Imagine that you just came home from a bad day at work. Then, you notice that a few things were misplaced, your partner has not yet made dinner, and there is unwashed laundry on the sofa.

So, to no surprise to anyone, you blow up. You might start with the typical "Am I the only who notices things here?!" and then proceed on a long tirade with increasing intensity, cadence, and profanity. To put it colorfully, you overreacted.

The best way to deal with your stress first is to control how you react to stressors. As you are about to blow your lid off, try replacing your increasingly negative thoughts with more rational ones. You might start rationalizing that maybe your housemates were busy or that the laundry had been there for a few minutes before your arrival. Any excuse would work so as long as your brain starts thinking that maybe, just maybe, you don't need to start yelling.

2. Always Plan for the "Difficult" Scenarios

One good practice you must maintain is identifying what scenarios tend to rustle your jimmies the most. Perhaps it's an angry customer. Or perhaps it's people misplacing stuff at home. Or being stuck in traffic next to a loud, obnoxious motorist.

Whatever sets you up, you have to identify it. This is so that you can prepare a script of sorts of what to do when you find yourself in that situation again. This way, you can let the raw emotions go over you while you maintain composure. Rehearse this script as often as you can, and you might find yourself becoming more refined with your angry outbursts.

3. Express Yourself (Positively)

This might be the most challenging aspect of your exercise but, whatever you do, refrain from performing any act or saying any statement that you will regret later on.

As you are about to go off, try to anchor yourself to that script you have made. Depending on your script, you might remove yourself from the room or start counting to ten. The goal here is to let that surge of high emotion go through you long enough for your more rational side to take control again.

In this aspect, it is also a good idea to address your aggressive tendencies. You might have a knack towards clutching something until it snaps, punching a wall, or dropping some F-bombs when you are angry. These are natural expressions of anger and stress, but they will leave a nasty impression on anyone who witnesses your outburst.

If possible, replace your aggressive actions with subtler and more positive actions to channel your rage through.

4. Deal with Resentment

Resentment can be best described as any lingering negative emotion you have over a situation or a person. If not addressed, it could progressively change the way you communicate around a certain person, group, or situation.

To deal with resentment, you have to accept the fact that everyone is different. What they do and how they choose to interact with you is beyond your control. As such, you should not be holding any negative feelings for things that you are not mostly responsible for. By addressing any lingering resentment, you can quickly move on to more pressing tasks and interactions in your schedule.

5. Maintain an "Anger Diary"

Writing things down can help you deal with your anger in two fronts. First, it's cathartic as you are pouring all your anger into something that is not destructive. And think about it, the only person who is going to get potentially hurt by what you just wrote is someone who would accidentally peruse your notes.

Second, writing taps into the more rational part of your brain. This means that you allow yourself to organize your thoughts and rationalize why things happened in that particular sequence. Thus, you can make a better judgment call and determine whether or not your anger was founded on something reasonable.

6. Use "I Feel" Statements

It is easy to get accusatory when you are angry. As such, you tend to start your statements with a "you," which can be perceived as a personal attack. Depending on the other person's personality, this could be the start of a conversation with an ever-escalating level of aggression.

Yes, there is no denying that you are angry, but you can be less abrasive about it with your choice of words. Start with something like "I feel" because this still validates your anger but does not attack the other person whatsoever. This way, they will be more open to what you have to say.

7. Always, Always Stick to the Subject

When angry, it is easy to go on a tirade where you list everything that has ticked you off to that point. However, this does not help with any conversation you have as anyone listening to you will now struggle in finding the context of what you are trying to say.

A lot of self-restraint is necessary here as you would want your listeners to exactly know what made you feel this way. Stick with the issue that is most relevant to the situation and refrain from digressing. The less you rant and rage, the quicker it is for people to understand what you are trying to communicate.

For Adversarial Relations

Let us say that you have a long-running confrontational relationship with someone. As such, both of you cannot properly hear each other and resort to being defensive, dismissive, and argumentative with each other.

In essence, dealing with your internal noise is no longer enough. Building trust with that long-standing thorn in your side must be done over a series of conversations.

To facilitate a healthy line of communication with special cases, you have to consider the following.

1. Write a Special Script

First, you have to identify which people you tend to have the most disagreements with in a room. Identify what they do or say that could set you off and what you, in turn, do and say that could set them off.

At the same time, try to anticipate what they feel and need in every conversation that you have with them and prepare some responses.

However, it is best that you do not assume what they want from that encounter. Your script should be something that, at the very least, accommodates what that person could possibly want out of you whenever they have to talk with you.

2. Explain

The best way to make a person trust you gradually is to be as transparent as possible. When you are the one approaching them, wave a proverbial white flag by stating why you want to talk with them. This, at the very least, gives them the signal that you come in peace.

As for your conversation, it is best that you stick to the facts and carefully lay out your proposal. And if you do find yourself getting incensed by their response, stick to your reasons without becoming too aggressive. And if things do fail, just say something like, “I respect your views, and I think it’s best that we stop here,” and ask them if they want to do this again later on. Perhaps cooler heads will prevail next time.

3. Take Turns

One good strategy in talking with a person you are predisposed to get angry at is to treat the entire conversation as a game of chess. No, this is not about the mind games (not outwardly, at least) but is all about letting each party finish a turn before the other makes a move.

This means that nobody is to interject while the other person is talking. Cutting a person off mid-sentence tends to be perceived negatively, which can escalate aggression. If possible, have another person facilitate the conversation, warning both parties to respect the other person's turn and signifying when they can say something in response.

It is a bit tedious and more demanding of a conversation, mind you. But it does help in ensuring that any anger does not surface and derail the entire dialogue for everyone.

To Summarize

There is no doubt that being under stress and getting angry is a lousy experience. However, it is not the sensation itself that sucks. Rather, it is the potential you have to create interpersonal conflict while in such a frenzied state. Then again, there are times when you have to talk to someone even when you are mad.

The primary strategy here is to do a bit of self-censoring. Get to the point immediately and say things in the most direct and passive of statements possible. Do it right, and you will not say anything regretful by the time your anger has finished its course through your system.

Chapter 6: Dealing with "Noise" Part 2: In Case of Miscommunication

"Well, it's really no use our talking in the way we have been doing if the words we use mean something different to each of us...and nothing."

-Malcolm Bradbury

Once you have dealt with your own "noise," the next part involves dealing with the noise coming from the transition of your ideas to the receiver. And this is where things get crucial as an improper delivery could lead to an entirely different (and mostly negative) outcome.

Miscommunication is rife in places where a constant need to convey information is necessary, like a workplace. The problem with miscommunicating, however, is not limited to the fact that the information was not received properly. It could also be the source of interpersonal conflicts which, in turn, prevents future healthy interactions.

As such, the remedy here is to avoid miscommunication. But how should you do it?

Why Does Miscommunication Occur?

The first thing that we have to address in this part is why we tend to miscommunicate. To do that, let us go back to your previous table.

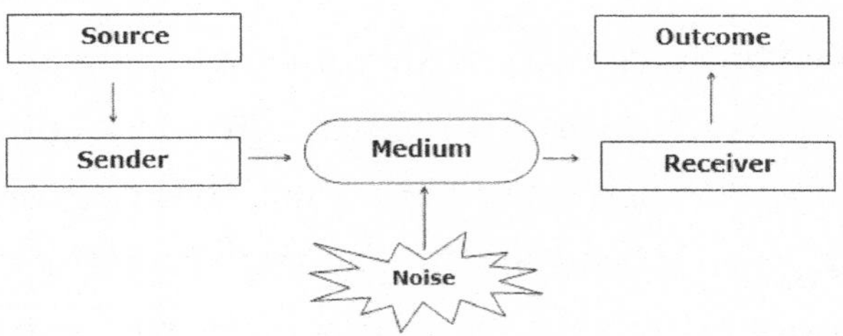

You might notice that the noise element is pointed directly at the medium, but make no mistake—that noise can appear in different nodes across the process.

To elaborate, here are some possible scenarios where miscommunication can occur.

1. The Wrong Source and Destination

For example, you tell someone in your workplace that he has to do something. But what if you have no authority to tell that person to do anything? The end result is that the person does nothing in response to the message.

Here is another scenario: what if you tell someone to do something but that something is not in that person's jurisdiction? Perhaps you are asking them to look at a report from production, but that person is in marketing. The end result is that the person would find someone else to do what you asked.

2. An Unspecified Message

In this aspect, the most common mistake is not specifying exactly what you want. For example, you told a subordinate to finish a report on something but failed to specify to whom it should be sent to (i.e., you). The result is that person would do the report and then submit it to the channels he usually sends his reports to but not directly to your office.

Or, more specifically, what if you never specified the period that the data to be processed should come from? Chances are that person will prepare an extensive report filled with data that you have no need for right now.

3. The Wrong Signal

What if you asked someone to buy you a book on Arizona's penal code but forgot to specify that it has to be the most recent edition of the author? That person would just grab a copy of whatever book fits your description, but you would not be happy because it is the wrong edition or the wrong book overall.

Or how about if you asked for a report but did not specify the format? The people you asked for that report would use the format they are most comfortable with or send you multiple formats of the same report.

4. The Wrong Medium

Here, you try to reach out to someone in a medium that they either don't use frequently or is inappropriate to the message. For example, you want to address a private matter to someone, but you sent it through the company mail.

Or, more commonly these days, you want to settle an issue with someone over social media but, instead of privately messaging them, you accidentally tagged their profile in a public post. In either case, the receiver would respond negatively to the message, no matter how good your intentions were.

5. Messaged Alter by Noise

This is all too common in electronic media. For example, you ask someone over a video call to prepare you a report, but a change in internet speeds caused that part of your message to get garbled.

Or, even more commonly, what if you meant for a person to do one thing, but you inadvertently typed out a command to do the other? Another common example here is if you intended to send a message to person A but tagged or sent it to person B or C instead.

In these scenarios, the message is either given a poor response or not responded to at all.

6. Wrong Reception

In this instance, the receiver successfully got the message. However, they failed to properly interpret it, resulting in the improper response.

For example, you are dating someone, and you proposed to them. They said "not now," much to your dismay. However, in your mind, they said "no." Technically, they insinuated for you do this again some time later, but your mind perceived the denial as one that involves the relationship, not the proposal itself. So, you misinterpreted the "not now" and got angry about it.

This is also common in the workplace when employees, too eager to please their superiors, might do something without going into the assignment details further. As such, they might do something with the wrong parameters.

Either way, what they did is not something that you exactly asked for.

Preventing Miscommunications

The most sensible thing that you could do is to make sure that you are properly understood to prevent any miscommunication. Here's how.

1. Be Clear and Concise

Differences in interpretation occur when parties fail to grasp the actual directives, provided that there were any given. It is important that you say what you want to say in the most direct manner possible and using the most common of terms.

Avoid speaking randomly or in circles so as not to baffle your audience. Also, digressing from the issue or giving away too many tiny details tends to confuse people as well.

If possible, set up a clear narrative of what you are saying. You can use a step-by-step module so people can easily connect the dots and do exactly what you are asking of them. The goal here is to make your message follow a simple, short, and clear line so that everyone is on the same page when trying to understand you.

2. Never, Ever, Assume

There is no bigger culprit to miscommunication than assuming. For instance, if you asked a person why he didn't do exactly what you asked, 90% of the time, his answer will be because he assumed that it was supposed to be done this way. Or you might assume that a person has understood your message in the way that you intended for it to be understood.

Assumption in communication occurs when all participants interpret things according to their own understanding and perspective. And since both parties failed to relay and interpret signals, conflict tends to arise from assuming.

Before ending a conversation, always ask if that person has fully grasped what you are asking of them. This way, if ever failure arises, the blame is not on you but on the person listening to you.

On the flip side, if you are the one listening, remember to do the active listening technique and take time to comprehend the core issue of the conversation along with the set of instructions given to you.

3. Adjust your Communication Style

As was stated, people have different ways of absorbing and processing information. Some people need to be instructed to the letter and do well working under specific guidelines. Others want to communicate via email and others through the phone or directly.

Others are best when they can receive instructions in writing while others can do with being told once. The point is that people eventually come to an understanding with you at their own pace and style.

Be mindful of the preferred style or medium that your audience has with receiving messages. From that point on, all you have to do is to re-mold your message so that it fits what they are used to the most.

4. Know that Text Media has its Limits

Text, emails, and other forms of electronic media are the most popular forms of communication now. However, they also tend to be the most problematic right now. You might be surprised at how entire relationships can be ruined just because of one poorly worded tweet or status update. Even entire careers and reputations went down in flames because of the things those people said online.

What you have to remember is that text has two disadvantages. First, it cannot carry the subtler elements of communications like nuance, context, and even sarcasm. Second, it has an element of perpetuity to it, so anything poorly-worded you say now will come back to haunt you in a few weeks or years.

The strategy here, then, is to think before you click. Make sure that your choice of words have been thoroughly thought out and your overall message leaves no room for interpretation, especially negative ones. If you check your message one to three times, then and only then can you send it to your intended audience.

5. Check and Follow Up

If the conversation is rather long, it might be a bit too pointless to ask them for clarification once and only at the ending. This is quite true in situations where you have to talk to multiple people over a long period of time, like in a class or a large symposium.

At every point of your talk, stop the conversation and ask whether or not they understood that part of your discussion. Also, ask them if there are any terms or directives that they do not understand properly. This will give them the chance to raise any questions that they have in mind and have the same answered, reaching an understanding with you.

One nifty trick you can do here is to do a summary. This allows you to go through every major point of the discussion without having to spend another hour or two explaining what has already been covered.

For situations when you are giving directives to people, make sure to do a follow-up. Check on them regularly to see how they are progressing and address any issue that they might have with the task as it progresses. A follow-up is your way of showing that you are willing to go above and beyond the call of duty to make sure that you and the person can reach an understanding.

A Miscommunication Recovery Plan

What happens, then, if there is a misunderstanding? Is that conversation a lost cause? Not really.

There is still a way to prevent a total breakdown of communication and clear up the misunderstanding. What it requires from you is the ability to act and adjust quickly.

Just remember that there is no hard and fast rule for recovering from misunderstandings. That being said, there are a few tips that you could easily apply in your interactions. Here are some of them:

1. Acknowledge the Breakdown

First and foremost, you have to quickly realize that things are not going the way you wanted them to happen. Nobody's getting what they wanted, and the entire dialogue is about to devolve into a shouting match.

You have to know at which point things are about to go awry so that you can immediately adopt a de-escalation stance. If you are fast enough, you can quickly pull the communication back to a more productive direction.

2. Set the Goalpost

In order to help the dialogue go back to something more conducive to an understanding, you have to have a guide. This is where a goal will come into play as it helps you direct your efforts in the communication, so everything remains productive.

In most cases, your goal in any communication is an understanding. Being vindicated, proven right, or even "winning" is not something that you ought to aim for unless, of course, you are in a debate or a trial. In every interaction you have, the goal is to always make that other person see your perspective and you of theirs.

Keep this goal in mind and you could guide every word that you say to make that relationship functional.

3. Find the Point of Failure

You have to also identify where exactly in the dialogue did things get out of hand. Was it something you said, or was it a gesture you made? Was it some throwaway quip you uttered that set the other person off?

Alternatively, what did that person say or do that started this problem? You have to find this exact point where the communication broke down so you can start fixing it. Perhaps you might want to apologize and say you did not mean what you said or did.

Once that point has been cleared up, your dialogue should go back to its original course as planned.

4. Behave Assertively

One other useful thing that you can do to prevent things from breaking down is to be mindful of your reactions towards anything offensive that the person might say. For example, if that person is criticizing your views or correcting you on your mistakes, the best that you could do is to remain objective and acknowledge their input.

What you should never do, on the other hand, is flare up and meet the aggression with your own aggression. This results in an escalation, which leads to conflict.

Undoubtedly, the ability to remain composed even as your opinions and character are being deconstructed in your face is a hard skill to learn. But it is eventually learned, and you can maintain at least a decent level of surface-level civility to keep your interpersonal relationships from breaking down further.

5. Do Not Let Others Join in on the Fight

When clearing up a misunderstanding, you should limit the involvement to you and the people that were directly tied to the incident. Do not let other people join in as they also have their own opinions, which could fan the flames of conflict even further.

Talk to the involved persons directly and, if possible, in a discreet place. More prying eyes lead to more miscommunication. And miscommunication does have a nasty habit of feeding on itself.

6. Be the Bigger Person

This is perhaps the most crucial lesson you will have to learn with conflict management; you are not infallible. Your opinions are not always right. Your advice is not always solicited. And your comments are not always tactful. You are human, after all, which means there is always a part of you that makes mistakes.

So, what you have to do is to own up to anything that you might have done to contribute to the misunderstanding instead of looking for something to blame. With your ego out of the way, the path towards a peaceful resolution is now clear.

To Conclude

The one element that will give you the most worry about miscommunication is its prevalence. It is surprisingly easy for people to misunderstand each other due to the high potential of failure at every point of the communication pathway. If one element is wrong or tampered by noise, then the outcome is not going to be to anyone's liking.

As such, you have to be mindful of every element in the communication process. Find out where a potential breakdown could occur and be quick enough to patch it up. If everything is done right, you could avoid a misunderstanding at best or prevent things from escalating further, at least.

Chapter 7: Dealing with "Noise" Part 3: Interactions in the Toxic Realm

"Sadly, whenever I make my opinions more important than the difficult people God made, I turn the wine back into water."

-Bob Goff

More often than not, the biggest problem you have to deal with is not the noise coming from the medium or yourself. It's the noise coming from the receiver. Perhaps they did not understand you fully, or they misinterpreted what you just said. Either way, a breakdown of communication is sure to happen.

The best part of dealing with noise coming from the receiver is that it is easy to handle so as long as you maintain a confident stance and stick to reason and logic. In time, you would win these people over and reach an understanding with them in every conversation.

But what if the receiver itself is not hindered by noise, but IS the noise? What if their personality is rather abrasive to the point of toxicity? Can you still get through a conversation with them without being run over? The answer is yes, and there are a few things that you have to keep in mind.

Wading through a toxic interaction can be difficult if you do not know who you are dealing with. Toxic people can come in any shape or size, but they often fall into six distinct categories.

What will follow is a series of descriptions of what forms a toxic person can take, what they can do to any conversation, and what you can do to deal with them.

The Naysayer

The most favorite word of this person is "No!" To them, that short, one-syllable utterance has so much power in the sense that it can cut off any dialogue short. And aside from any interaction, their statements could even dissuade you from doing anything you have planned for yourself.

You have a good idea? Too bad, it's not going to work. You're going to college? Tough luck, you'll quit in a semester or two. How's that new job of yours? I heard it's not paying much. And so on and so forth.

Whether they are aware of it or not, the naysayer's primary export is negativity of varying scale and intensity. That does not mean, however, they are ill-willed towards you. They are just inclined to look at life through highly cynical glasses, leading to a rather dour world view.

How to Deal with Them

More often than not, naysayers have something to contribute and are generally concerned about how you are going to pull things off. So, it is best to let this inner desire shine through their abrasive negativity.

Start by acknowledging their concerns. Say something like, "thank you for your perspective. I do appreciate your concern for me/this project." Now, their negativity is disarmed as the focus now shifts from their comments to their intentions.

Next, you will have to make their intentions actionable. Say something like, "What do you have in mind?" Now, the spotlight is on them to add something to enhance your proposition.

The Complainer

The difference between a naysayer and a complainer is similar to the difference between a word and a sentence. Where the naysayer says one or a few comments of negativity, the complainer makes a litany of them.

Propose something, and the complainer will tell you five to ten instances why it is wrong and where everything could go wrong. Is there enough budget for this? What about working schedules? All of you are busy enough, so why did management give you this extra burden? Now, they'll have to cancel their schedules for this! And the list goes on.

Another notable element with the complainer is their ability to build momentum. If left to their own devices, their list of worries can increase in intensity. Some of their fears are even so prospective that they could border on the irrational.

How to Deal with Them

What you will have to understand about complainers is that they are merely venting their frustrations. They are not there to sour the mood for everybody else, at least, not intentionally. This means that it is best to let everything out of their system.

The trick here is where you should let them vent their feelings. If possible, let them do it with you in private. This allows you to discuss such issues with them extensively without putting the group's discussion on hold.

Once they have cooled down and the rational part of their brain kicks in, they can start focusing on addressing actual problems with actual solutions.

The Shifter

If there was any person in a group that could quickly make a conversation veer off course, it is the shifter. The game plan of the shifter is rather ingenious. All they have to do is to participate and then contribute to the discussion. Shifters are one of the more active communicators out there.

This is where things get tricky; they might add some comments here and there and raise some questions, but whatever they contribute is not relevant to the discussion at all. Soon enough, you will find that your discussion has drifted far away from the core topic. At their worst, the shifter can generate a lot of discussions, but ones that tend to not answer the primary issue you raised.

How to Deal with Them

Make no mistake. A lot of shifters mean well. The only problem they have is that whatever they have to bring serves no actual purpose to the conversation at hand.

The best way to deal with a shifter is to always ask for a point of order. If the shifter starts raising an issue while another is still active, say something like, "Thank you for the comment. To help in the discussion, please elaborate on how it ties to what we are trying to cover here?"

If that sounds a bit patronizing, then you might need some creativity on your part. Let us say that what the person raised is an issue that will be covered later on, partly or exactly. You could say something like, "That's a great observation. You've figured out something we are going to cover later!"

In both cases, you are trying to give the shifter the help they need to reorganize their thoughts without humiliating them in public.

The Nitpicker

There is no doubt that getting the details right is important, but the nitpicker obsesses over the minutiae to the point of aggravation. Unlike the naysayer who shoots your ideas wholesale, the nitpicker will be the one to strike at every minute point or detail you raised in the hopes of disarming your argument.

Let us say, for example, that you are arguing with a nitpicker. Suddenly, they criticize you for what you just said because it's the wrong noun or because your grammar is atrocious. Soon enough, you'll be defending your entire argument in depth.

The nitpicker is common in group interactions. They'd be the first to pick up any flaw in your idea and wave it around like a prospector finding gold. If left to their devices, a nitpicker can derail any conversation more than what a shifter could ever hope to achieve.

How to Deal with Them

The goal of the nitpicker is rather simple: Triumph over their opponents by exposing the flaws in their ideas. It can be petty, but it can also be used on more productive channels.

To do this, you have to make the nitpicker see the bigger picture. When they start scrutinizing the smallest of details, it is your responsibility to snap them back to their senses. Say something like, "Point taken. But first, let us do things step by step."

Or, if you are in an argument with them, say something like, "Noted. Now, let's get back on point." The goal here is to stop the nitpicker from obsessing over the details so that you can quickly go through the entire proposition first.

But do extend an olive branch to these people by assuring them that their observations will be taken into consideration later on. You could even make them a resource person to help you in future projects.

The "Yes" Man

Eager to please but always failing to deliver, the yes man is someone who wants to fit in in any group or organization. They want to make a good impression, so they agree to any proposition or request you give despite their limitations.

For instance, you request a yes man to do something, and they agree to it. While doing what you asked for, another person asks the yes man to do something, and they agree to it. Then, another person asks the yes man to do something, and they agree to it. And the pattern continues.

There is no doubt that their intentions are noble but, more often than not, they run the risk of overwhelming themselves. At collaborative efforts, this results in something called bottlenecking, where work has to be stopped because one part (or person, in this regard) has gotten clogged up.

How to Deal with Them

The yes man means well, which is why you'd rather be compassionate with them instead of being argumentative. What you should do to a yes man is encourage them to be as honest and transparent as possible.

Naturally, they'd not do this on their own, which is why you should prod them with some hints here and there. When you ask them to do something, clarify first if their schedule allows for your task. If they say yes, follow up with a question like, "How much time will this need to be finished?" or "Do you have any other task that needs to be done?" or the ever-potent "What do you need to get this task done quickly?"

The goal here is to make the yes man determine for himself whether or not what you are proposing is something that they are amenable with. With all options laid out, the yes man can chart a better course for themselves while still feeling that they are already accepted in the group.

The Tank

The tank is the epitome of pushy and aggressive behavior. When this person comes through, they'll push their ideas and commands at anyone without any consideration as to what that person feels and thinks. For the tank, it's their way or the highway.

But the tank's bossiness and domineering bravado is not them at their most lethal. The tank loves a fight and will absolutely demolish the opposition through sheer force and a louder, shriller voice. They might even goad others to oppose them for the thrill of it. Once they are done with you, you will feel defeated and confused as to what the hell just happened.

One other element that makes the tank deadly is their relationship with you, professional or otherwise. Perhaps they are your boss or your close friend. They might even be your partner, much to your dismay.

Tanks often occupy the topmost positions in any group due to their personality or were made into tanks because of their position. Either way, you can't just do away with the tank without experiencing some serious consequences in your career and personal life.

How to Deal with Them

The only way you are going to survive the tank's onslaught is to be methodical and calm as much as you can. First is that you have to brace yourself. Look at them in the eye as they are about to deliver a verbal beatdown. Manage your breathing and temper here as you want to be as calm as possible when the tank is delivering their verbal payload.

As the tank starts belting out their opinions, you must interrupt their attack. You can do this by slowly saying their name over and over again until you get their attention. The goal here is to slowly increase the tone of your voice so the tank can get the idea that you mean business.

After you have stopped the tank dead in their tracks, now is the time to aim and fire. The goal here is to reinforce your bottom line with the right words. Use phrases like "From my viewpoint" or "The way I see it." Do not use "I feel" or "I think" statements because that gives the tank new ammunition to fire at you, restarting their attack.

Once you delivered your line (as calmly and assertively as possible), let the tank have the last word. They might berate you more but, now, they'd look foolish being the only one yelling throughout the exchange.

However, do not close the door on them just yet. Give the tank the opportunity to discuss this matter with you later on.

To Conclude

What makes these people difficult to communicate with is not their personality. At least, not technically speaking.

If you think about it, these personalities do bring something of value to the conversation and the relationship. Naysayers, complainers, and nitpickers do help us ground our ambitions and aim for something more realistic and achievable.

Shifters help you explore other avenues to your ideas, giving you access to an even bigger picture than what you originally envisioned. Lastly, tanks and yes men do aim for results that help in motivating people to get things done.

What makes any relationship or interaction with them potentially toxic is in the application of such personalities. In general, they are seen as difficult people because their egos, methodologies, and overall behavior comes at the expense of a good conversation and a chance to build better relationships.

Your goal in communicating with them, then, is not to change how they think or act, but channel all that toxicity into more productive methods. You will find that, with the right re-calibration, these individuals can offer something valuable to you and you to them in return.

Chapter 8: Having a Great Public Presentation

"Public Speaking is the art of diluting a two-minute idea with a two-hour vocabulary."

-John F. Kennedy

More often than not, it is speaking in front of an audience where your skills as a communicator will be tested. In fact, you absolutely dread or loathe the idea of having to go up in front of many people, say your piece, and deal with the consequences from that act later.

But knowing how to speak in public is not only easy if you get the basics. It can be even beneficial for you in improving your own skills and make money off it in the end. It could even be a platform where you could sell your ideas and increase your network of contacts.

All of this can be yours if you master the basics of giving a good public presentation. And here's how:

Preparing your Speech

Every good performance out there starts with a script which is, in this regard, your speech. Writing a speech is basic enough in concept. All you have to do is prepare a monologue where your major points are contained and written in a linear, narrative fashion.

It is in the methodology where things get tricky. If you're not careful, you will end up with something boring. If you try too hard, you end up with something pointless.

As such, you must remember a few tips when writing your speech.

1. Know Your Audience

Before anything else, you have to know who you are presenting yourself to. Each audience member has their own needs and expectations, and you must meet those to the best of your abilities.

When preparing your speech, ask the following questions:

- Who is going to listen to my speech?
- What problems do they have that I can solve?
- Are there any considerations about my listeners that I also need to address as well?

For example, if you are speaking in front of a group of doctors, professionals, and academic experts, your presentation is going to be a bit more formal. But if you are talking to regular folks, teenagers, and college students, perhaps a bit more excitement and formality in your message's content will help you.

2. Choose a Topic

The subject matter of your presentation should be relevant to the questions you have answered in the previous section. If, for example, your audience expects to learn more about how they are going to close deals, then your topic may revolve around advanced negotiating or sales techniques.

But choosing a topic is the easy part. Now, you will have to give your presentation structure. Depending on the topic, a presentation can last for half an hour to no more than three. Regardless of the allotted time, your presentation should follow a structured narrative.

For solution-centric presentations (ones like "How to…" or something similar), they should follow a sequence like this.

1. State the Problem

2. Support with Facts

3. Present the Solution

4. Support with Strategies

5. Integrate

6. Conclude

You could even use the basic storytelling sequence for your presentation, which is as follows:

1. Setup

2. Conflict

3. Middle Point

4. Climax

5. Resolution

Also, do not overwhelm your audience with too much information. Just cover the basics of your chosen topic so that your audience can remember a point or two once your presentation is over.

3. Research

It is important that you sound as authoritative as possible when presenting your ideas. This means that you sound like you have mastered the topic well and are more than able to take on any question in the latter portion of your presentation.

This means that you have to research intently on every piece of information relevant to your topic. If possible, you have to cover every angle regarding the subject matter so you would not be blindsided with a question you have no prepared answer for.

4. Write it Down

Once you have the subject matter, the structure, and information, you have to write things down. Here are some tips to remember when creating your speech:

- **Start with an outline:** The outline serves as an introduction of sorts to your audience as to what they can expect to learn from your presentation. On your part, it helps you make the structure of your speech even more tangible so you could easily follow it.
- **Be conversational:** You should write your speech in the same style that you talk. You can even add some small talk here and there and some jokes if it helps in easing the tension between you and your audience.
- **Set up some speaker notes:** These are mini "cue cards" that help you deliver important parts of your presentation. Have

them placed anywhere that you can see but beyond the sight of the audience.

- **KISS (Keep it Short and Simple)**: Use short sentences and be specific as possible in your speech. It's not as if you have to recite that material word for word, anyway.

5. Bring Some Aids with You

Now, your presentation is not going to be as memorable if you don't use some visuals to get the attention of your audience. While preparing your speech, you should also set up a PowerPoint presentation using the major points in your discussion. Be as visual as possible here, using graphs, images, and other visual media to drive your point across to the audience.

It would also be a good idea to spend a bit on printing handouts. These will summarize your discussion and guide the listener through your presentation and after it.

Delivery

Now that you have everything needed for your presentation, all that is left to do is to deliver it. This is rather crucial as you will only have one chance to do this presentation. This only means that you have to make a good impression.

To do that, there are a few tips that you must remember:

1. Do Not Read

If you can, memorize your presentation. And if you can't, you can always use your speaker notes or your prepared speech.

What is to be avoided here is to show that you are reading from something while conveying your ideas. Audiences will know if you are reading because your head is lowered and your eyes are fixed on something.

Just memorize your speech as much as you can and refer only to your material if you get stuck. And if you do find yourself getting stuck, there is always the option to improve (more on this later). The audience wouldn't know that you are fumbling if you know how to recover quickly from a blunder.

2. Practice

So how do you memorize your speech and prevent yourself from going off-script? The answer is to practice your material.

Spend the few days before the presentation going through your material. It helps you feel calm, get comfortable with your presentation, and find out how you can refine your script to fit with the time allotted to you.

3. Dress for the Occasion

It goes without saying that you have to look your best but do not overdress to the point of being uncomfortable. A suit and tie combo are enough, but some speakers nowadays opt for more "casual" attire in the vein of Steve Jobs or Mark Zuckerberg.

Either way, if you are not sure, ask the event organizer what the expected attire will be of the audience. This way, you can match what you are wearing with their overall getup to be as comfortable when delivering your speech.

4. Mind Your Posture

Try to act as naturally as you can but maintain control over your body's movements. Stand straight and keep your head up so as to control your nerves and breathe regularly.

And even if you do make some mistakes, keep on going. Nobody but you would know that you've made a mistake so as long as you don't show it.

5. Have Some Enthusiasm

The one thing that you will have to remember is that excitement is contagious. With the right amount of enthusiasm, a speaker can build hype for any subject matter, even boring and complicated ones.

One great example of this is Carlos Matos, who presented BitConnect to an audience in the late 2010s. The offer itself can be dubious in hindsight now and the premise boring, but the way Matos draws up hype as he sings, yells, and builds on his energy in front of hundreds of people is effective, if not memorable.

Here's the video if you want to watch how he drums up interest for a premise that would have otherwise bored people out of their minds:

https://www.youtube.com/watch?v=vabXXkZjKiw.

The point is that if you are excited about the topic, your audience will be as well.

Common Public Speaking Pitfalls

Even with the right preparation and the right setup for good delivery, there is still that chance that you are going to muck up the execution of your presentation.

There is the off-chance that factors beyond your control were not to your favor for that instance. But, for most of the time, it is because you tend to commit some of the most common public presentation mistakes. They include, but are not limited to, the following.

1. Being Too Intelligent-Sounding

It is your goal to be as authoritative as possible when presenting your topic. However, you also run the risk of becoming too "intellectually oriented."

A lot of smart people often commit this mistake and sometimes unintentionally. Their choice of words are too advanced for common folk, their content lacks that emotional involvement, and the tone of their message is too stern or with no passion at all.

Your presentation should have a balance between factual information and emotional investment. Do not forget to add some personal tangents here and there so people can get a glimpse of the person behind the presentation. A joke or two is also good to ease the tension, especially if you have mastered the art of being funny.

And, most important of all, you have to establish that correlation that whatever idea or solution you're presenting will affect the audience on a personal level.

2. Getting Stiff

Think of it this way: why are you so comfortable talking with five to ten friends, but you immediately freeze in front of strangers of the same quantity? The source of your problem, then, is not the number of people but your overall level of comfort in them.

It is easy to spot a nervous presenter because their body language is stiff as if somebody glued their elbows and knees shut. However, you can easily remedy this by constantly rehearsing your piece and preparing for every possible query or response.

Use a camera or a mirror so you could see what you are doing as you are delivering that message in your rehearsals. Correct any physical and verbal tic you make and find a way to release all that tension in your upper body. If you are comfortable with your message now, the chances of you successfully delivering your presentation has increased.

And speaking of verbal tics...

3. Filler

When we talk about filler, we are referring to those seemingly inconsequential phrases we utter before, during, and after every sentence we say. Here are some of the most popular fillers in the English language.

Sounds	Phrases	Words
Um	I think....	Okay
Hmm	You know?	So
Uh	What I am trying to say is...	Like
Er	You see...	Basically
Mm-hmm	I mean...	Actually
Uh-huh	At the end of the day...	Literally
	Believe me...	Seriously
	I suppose	Essentially
		Quite
		Reasonably

	Kind of/Kinda It is what it is... Or something Stuff like that	Well Honestly

Fillers tend to happen because your brain is trying to catch up with the speed of your mouth. They are essentially non-silent pauses so your brain can reorganize itself and continue with the presentation.

They only become problematic if their frequency increases. Some unprepared speakers even have three to four filler words and phrases for a single sentence, which breaks immersion.

Again, your remedy here is to practice your material. Internalizing the points of your presentation and mastering the cues you have set up can help you prevent your presentation from being filled with too many unnecessary pauses.

4. A Lame Opening

How you start your presentation can make or break the entire endeavor. A common bad habit among public speakers is to meander in their first parts. They might tell a joke, or ramble for several seconds, or apologize profusely for some bad attempt at self-deprecation. All of these tend to fail at getting the attention of the audience.

To avoid this, open your presentation with a bang. You don't have to do something bombastic, mind you. What you need is a good pitch.

Start with some engaging story or tell a startling statistic. Better yet, open your presentation with a thought-provoking question. These tend to get your audience's attention right from the start and should give you a foundation where you can keep them hooked for the duration of your presentation.

5. "Any Questions?"

Most speakers think that this is a good end to their presentation but, in truth, it is not. There are two reasons for this. First, it invites you to a lot of backtracking and deviation, especially if an audience member asks a far-off question.

Second, your audience is still processing everything that you have said. So, more often than not, they don't have any questions that you need to answer. And if you do a Q&A while they are still processing information, you are bound to end your presentation with a dud.

Instead of a Q&A, end your presentation with a call to action and then a closing statement. You can do an open mic period right before ending things. This way, you end your presentation with high energy.

Storytelling Tips

Storytelling is one of the better strategies you could use to get your audience emotionally invested in what you are trying to say. The reason for this is that a story has everything that a person could want from a narration. It has information, it has that emotional appeal, and it has a sequence that helps people correlate one different idea to another.

The opportunity to tell a story can happen at any moment. As such, you should learn how to tell one effectively, and the tips below will help you.

1. Hit the Curiosity Gap

A lot of salespeople get the attention of their audience by opening their pitch with a question. Let us say that you are invited to talk about passive income to college students.

You could say something like, "What If I told you that you could earn money while you are still getting your degree? And what if you could earn this money without doing anything else extra?"

And right at that instance, you have gotten the attention of your audience. To hit that curiosity gap, you have to know the needs of the audience and present them with a situation that they are familiar with.

2. VAK

VAK simply means Visual, Audio, and Kinesthetic modalities in your line delivery and is a strategy used by psychologists and therapists to make listeners do what they are saying.

This technique works by helping your listeners put up a "mental picture" of what you are trying to say. If you are just saying stuff without any passion, your listeners could not make that mental picture and thus cannot connect with your presentation.

This is where changes in your tone and the delivery of your line could help you. Visual aids like pictures and videos can also help you here. Even if you are talking about something bland, changes in your VAK modalities can help your audience get emotionally invested in your story.

3. Introduce Conflict and Resolution

The two traditional storytelling elements that you have to get right are conflict and resolution. This is because every person out there is familiar with adversity and knows that solutions are the best workaround to anything adverse that they counter.

To do this, always identify a problem and one that your audience can relate to. One mistake that presenters often make is just looking at their presentation from their own perspective or that of their team's. As such, the entire thing could be self-serving or highly intellectual.

You could prevent this by re-framing the way you present your idea to the audience. Bring to their attention a problem that they know and have your ideas provide the solution to that problem.

4. Appeal to their Ego

You have to understand that everyone in that audience is there for personal reasons. So why not leverage that self-focused motivation in crafting your story? The one thing about stories like the ones Aesop makes is that they are too "preachy." They tell good lessons, there's no doubt about that, but they always talk to the audience from a certain moral high ground.

Do not do this and, instead, use your stories as a bridge between a person and the solution to their problem. Think of it this way; your stories are going to be more relatable if the endpoint involves your audience learning how to triple their earnings, master the basics of photography, or any other thing that you were proposing at the start of your presentation.

To Summarize

There is no doubt that public presentation or speaking engagements are nerve-wracking experiences. The fact that you only have one chance to pull it off successfully and that there is a wide margin of error only puts more pressure on your part to get things right.

Before accepting any speaking engagement, you should have set up a system where you can prepare, research, and rehearse your material. At the same time, you must plan for every deviation to your script and set up different fallbacks in the event that they pop up in your discussion.

Then, you have to make yourself comfortable with the prospect of presenting your ideas, feelings, and thoughts to a lot of people. And, in some cases, you must even come to terms with the fact that your presentation will generate a lot of pushback and scrutiny from the public.

And, most important, you have to keep telling yourself that whatever happens from your public presentation will not harm you; at least not directly. And with that, you might start getting comfortable with the concept of presenting yourself before the masses on a regular basis.

Chapter 9: Feedback: How to Give and Respond to It

"Criticism, like rain, should be gentle enough to nourish a Man's growth without destroying his roots."

-Frank A. Clark

Whether we like it or not, feedback is part of our day-to-day communication. It cannot be helped that a major part of our interactions with people revolve around responding to what they said, how they look, and what they are proposing.

As such, the ability to give feedback is an essential skill to master. But an even more important skill is in receiving it and acting on it in the healthiest manner possible.

Feedback and Your Brain

What exactly happens inside your head when we receive feedback? Chances are that you already feel bad for something that you did, but it is even harder to hear the same thoughts being voiced by others.

And why is this so? Neuroscience tells us that the brain is designed to be a rather protective organ in the sense that it will prioritize its own welfare over others, whether you are aware of it or not.

In essence, it goes out of its way to protect you from negativity and make you feel that you are in the right, even if clearly you are not.

How it works is quite simple: Almost all types of feedback are viewed by the brain as criticism, and criticism, in itself, is perceived as an external threat.

To help you understand this concept better, here's Abraham Maslow's Hierarchy of Needs.

Generally speaking, criticism attacks the upper tiers of the hierarchy, namely self-actualization and esteem. But, for the brain, it feels like it is attacking the lower tiers (i.e., the ones primarily focused on basic survival).

Here's an example: Let us say that you had presented a report and one of your audience members says something like, "Hey, your report had a lot of errors. I couldn't agree with what you were saying because of those."

To them, they were just saying that you need to do more research on your report before presenting it. To you, more often than not, they just attacked your very being and seemingly made your contributions to the group worthless.

One other thing about negativity is that it is retained easier on the brain but often done so inaccurately. An off-hand comment can be remembered as a serious insult or a request to do better as a personal attack depending on your mind frame in that instant.

This is what is called a negativity bias. Our brains tend to process negative feedback more than the positive but in a way that hinders proper development and communication.

Finding a workaround for this bias, then, is important in learning how to give and receive feedback.

Offering Feedback

A. Mind Your Purpose

For what particular reason are you giving that feedback? What is your primary goal in telling something to a person who needs to hear it? Here is a list of some of the negative and positive motivations behind giving people feedback that they need to hear.

Positive	**Negative**
• Concern for another • A sense of responsibility for that person • Guidance • Support • Encouragement • Discipline	• To lash out • To defend or deflect your behavior • To demoralize • Appeasement for another party • To make the person inferior

It goes without saying that the more positive motivations can result in better-worded feedback. However, just make sure that whatever feedback you give reflects that actual reason as to why you are giving it in the first place.

2. Focus on the Act, not the Actor

A crucial step to learn here is to always separate the person from his actions. In essence, try to focus on correcting the action and not the character of the person when giving criticism.

This will separate the person from the situation that they put themselves in. It's not that they are stupid or idiotic or evil, it's just that they did something not exactly good in that instance. This way, they can focus on what you are trying to say without being personally insulted.

3. Give a Criticism Sandwich

A method popularized by Cosmetics mogul Mary Kay Ash, the criticism sandwich is feedback that gives a more comprehensive "review" of a person's actions and the situations that they are in. In essence, you give them a detailed appraisal of what just happened so that your feedback will not be seen as entirely negative.

The criticism sandwich follows this sequence:

A. Start with a positive comment

B. Focus on the strong points of the person

C. Support with complements

D. Give the criticism

E. Remind the person of their strong points

F. End on a positive note.

Let us say, for this example, that an employee of yours named Bobby went out and sealed a deal with a client without notifying you first. Perhaps you wanted to talk with that client yourself and had prepared a presentation, but one of your own just did it but without your consent.

Giving a criticism sandwich should sound like this:

"Bobby, thank you for what you did (**positive comment**). Had you not acted this way (**strong point**), we would not have sealed such a deal with that client. Thank you very much (**compliment**).

But next time, please notify me or your team of any interaction you will initiate with our clients. We work as a team and we should communicate as one (**criticism**). But, despite that, you did good and your initiative really helped the team! **(strong point)**

Rest assured that our bosses and we appreciated what you did. You might even have saved your team a lot of time and money in convincing the client to close the deal. Drinks are on me tonight! **(end on a positive note**)."

You could even make the criticism even less stinging if you phrase it positively. Say something like "I would really love if you..." or "You could really do a great job if you..." or "The one thing that will make this even greater than it is is if you..." If done right, you could prevent a lot of toxicity from leaking into your dialogue with that person.

Receiving Feedback

1. Build up an Immunity

What stings the most with feedback is the fact that it almost always catches us off-guard. You could prevent this by asking for feedback as often as possible, especially with the people that you trust.

How you could do this is rather easy. Before you do anything, ask some open-ended questions like the following:

- If you can make two or three suggestions on how I could have done things better, what would they be?
- Is there a better way for me to handle that situation?
- Do you know of a way to make my job easier?
- If you were in my position now, would you have done things differently?

Asking these questions frequently puts you on a direct path towards receiving feedback. As such, you tend to get less offended if people voice their concerns about you.

On the other hand, these questions immediately put the other person in a position where they can add value to the conversation. They can now comment on what you did without fear of repercussions from your side.

2. Take time to Reflect

The one thing that you shouldn't do is respond immediately to feedback. The reason for this is that humans tend to "explain away" what they did, which is seen as a rather defensive move.

Let the person finish their feedback and listen intently. Once they have said their piece, reflect on what was said. You could even do multiple reflections for the same feedback before you respond to it.

The goal here is to get the essence of what they are saying and what they want out of that feedback. If you understand this, your response will be more effective.

3. Embrace Your Mistakes and Grow

It is hard to admit to our mistakes, which is why receiving feedback is often next to impossible. More often than not, we blame our mistakes on external factors like the weather, the setup of the system, and even other people.

The idea of embracing your failures, however, has become a more prevalent concept these days. There is something so liberating and endearing with admitting that you are capable of mucking it up. And, if you do embrace your faults and mistakes, feedback that was intended to demoralize hurts less for you now.

But knowing that you make mistakes is not enough. You also have to give the assurance that you are working on ironing out the kinks in your personality, methodology, and any other aspect in your life that invites criticism. Once that assurance is given, all that is left to do is to show that such changes are taking place.

The Bottom Line

More often than not, it is the way we provide and receive feedback that is problematic, not the content itself. Your biggest problem here will always be your perceptions. It is either you don't think too much of what the other person feels when you provide feedback or overthink the feedback you received.

This is why your personal barriers are the biggest hurdles you will have to clear in order to communicate properly. Take the time to plan what you have to say before saying them so the person receives it in a manner that is healthy.

On the flip side, you also must curb your tendencies towards perceiving feedback negatively. Unless it is out in the open that that person hates the fact that you exist, do not assume negative intent for everything that they throw against you. With your negativity bias dealt with, you can easily go through life without accidentally offending people by the way you interact with them or getting needlessly offended yourself.

Chapter 10: Conclusion

Effective communication is 20% what you know and 80% how you feel about what you know."

-Jim Rohn

After everything you have learned from here, the one question that you may want to ask is this:

How should I know if I've become a better communicator?

The first thing that you have to look for is an ability to balance between talking and listening. More often than not, we tend to focus on getting the former right and disregard the latter. And then there are those that prefer to stay by the sidelines and not actively contribute to the conversation. Striking a balance between your ability to express and receive information can help you engage more with people.

The second ability is to not pay attention to your biases and presumptions too much. A lot of miscommunication occurs because we assume one thing over the other when it comes to people and how they think and feel. Being self-aware of how your actions can negatively affect others can help foster a clearer line of communication at home or work and prevent any sort of toxicity from coming out in your relationships.

Lastly, you become aware of how every move you make can be perceived by others. Every comment you utter, the body language and verbal tics that you make, and the way you present your ideas all play a role in how people perceive you. Thus, you become more mindful of the words that you say and the non-verbal cues that you give out when interacting with people.

With these elements, you are bound to develop one of the most important abilities that all sapient beings tend have: the ability to create connections with others wherever they go.

And how would you know that you already have these abilities? You don't. Or, technically speaking, you won't unless you actively apply all that you have learned here in your day-to-day interactions.

Thank you for taking the time to go through the entire book. I hope that you have learned all that you can about communicating your thoughts and ideas to other people. All that is left to do now is to start working on improving your communication skills following the strategies laid out in this book. Over time, you will be able to improve your relationships with the people that surround you.

Thank you

Before you go, I just wanted to say thank you for purchasing my book.

You could have picked from dozens of other books on the same topic, but you chose this one.

So, a HUGE thanks to you for getting this book and for reading all the way to the end.

Now, I want to ask you for a small favor. **Could you please consider posting a review? Reviews are one of the easiest ways to support the work of independent authors.**

This feedback will help me continue to write the type of books that will help you get the results you want. If you enjoyed it, please let me know!

Lastly, don't forget to grab a copy of your free bonus book "*Bulletproof Confidence Checklist.*" If you want to learn how to overcome shyness and social anxiety and become more confident, this book is for you.

Made in the USA
Las Vegas, NV
30 December 2023

83718008R00114